The Man Who Made
Mark Twain
Famous

Stories from the Kennedy Center, the White House, and Other Comedy Venues

Cappy McGarr

SAVIO
REPVBLIC

A SAVIO REPUBLIC BOOK
An Imprint of Post Hill Press
ISBN: 978-1-63758-167-4
ISBN (eBook): 978-1-63758-168-1

The Man Who Made Mark Twain Famous:
Stories from the Kennedy Center, the White House, and Other
Comedy Venues
© 2021 by Cappy McGarr
All Rights Reserved

Cover Design by Cody Corcoran
Cover Illustration by Mark Ulriksen

posthillpress.com
New York • Nashville
Published in the United States of America
1 2 3 4 5 6 7 8 9 10

For Janie, Elizabeth, and Kathryn.
You are the most selfless people in the world.
Now please enjoy this book about me.

NOTICE

"Persons attempting to find a motive in this narrative will be prosecuted; persons attempting to find a moral in it will be banished; persons attempting to find a plot in it will be shot."

—Mark Twain, *The Adventures of Huckleberry Finn*

CONTENTS

FOREWORD
by Ken Burns

as Mark Twain the first American comedian? In Huck Finn's words, "that ain't no matter." Whether you call him a comedian, a humorist, a satirist, or an apocryphal quote generator, the influence Twain's work has had on American literature and American comedy is unparalleled.

In his time, Twain was practically synonymous with humor, considered the funniest man on earth. But he wasn't just remarkable because he was funny.

One reason Twain was so influential is the very same reason he could make people laugh to begin with: he perfectly captured an emerging, authentic American voice and reflected enduring American contradictions in a way that no writer before him had quite been able to do. And he fearlessly satirized American institutions—from slavery, which he abhorred, to Congress, which he relentlessly mocked. He also understood the true origin of our laughter. He said, "The secret source of humor itself is not joy but sorrow. There is no humor in heaven."

In that way, his work accomplished a feat that is fundamental to all successful laugh-getters: he expressed complicated ideas a vast audience could relate to (i.e., none of us gets out of here alive), but that no one else had thought—or dared—to put on paper or say aloud. He studied *us* and mastered the American way of speaking and thinking, reproduced it flawlessly, and weaved in his own sharp-witted perspective along the way. My favorite one-liner of his is: "It's not that the world is filled with fools; it's just that lightning isn't distributed right."

That's exactly what American comedy does at its best. The people who make us laugh the most are those who have mastered the American language and life's sometimes cruel ironies—not just the words, but the gestures, the references, the subtleties.

And, like Twain, the most influential comedians go a step further. They don't just reflect our sensibilities; they refract them, questioning our assumptions about the world, undercutting the people in power, and puncturing pretension where they see it...which is everywhere.

So, it is perfectly fitting that America's highest honor for achievement in humor would be named for Mark Twain.

The Kennedy Center Mark Twain Prize for American Humor celebrates the American comedic tradition that I think arguably began with Twain himself. And it honors some of the finest modern storytellers who—in satirizing our politics, commenting upon our culture, and sharing their own unique experiences—are continuing his legacy.

Appropriately, the Mark Twain Prize also gives contemporary humorists an opportunity to cross paths with an American president—something Twain did on multiple occasions, from his unlikely friendship with Ulysses S. Grant to his adversarial relationship with Theodore Roosevelt.

Where the Mark Twain Prize commemorates the history of American comedy, this book, *The Man Who Made Mark Twain Famous*, commemorates the history of the Mark Twain Prize. And it does so through the inimitable drawl and laser wit of my friend Cappy McGarr, who co-founded the award and has been one of its most stalwart supporters for decades—in fact, since its inception.

I met Cappy when we sat together on the National Archives Foundation Board in the early 2000s. Quite literally, we sat next to each other—which made me the lucky one-man audience to Cappy's quips, asides, and uncanny impressions of every president since JFK.

Since then, we've shared a wonderful friendship that has spanned many years (and countless jokes).

Reading Cappy's book is not unlike sitting down to dinner with him and listening to the stories he has picked up from decades of rubbing elbows with political leaders and comedians alike. There are historic set pieces. There are laughs and howls and chuckles and chortles. There are names dropped, picked back up, and then shamelessly dropped again.

But more than that, Cappy has chronicled each and every Mark Twain Prize ceremony from the very beginning—effectively giving us a personal tour of the hall of fame for today's would-be Twains.

The last couple of decades of American politics have reminded us how desperate we are for figures like Twain, who can make sense of our absurd tragedies—and tragic absurdities—and, in response, create incisive, hilarious works that offer us some catharsis and release. Through the Mark Twain Prize, Cappy has helped pay tribute to nearly two dozen comedians who are filling Twain's shoes (and suit, and mustache) during these fraught times.

Along with the history of the Mark Twain Prize, Cappy has also shared another uniquely American story: that of his own life. His Texas upbringing; his courtship with his future wife, Janie; his earliest encounters with the political juggernaut known as LBJ; his journey to the board of the Kennedy Center; his visits to, and shows hosted from, the White House. He's a wisecracking southerner who has somehow charmed his way into encounters with some of the most influential people of his time. Who better then to tell the story of the Mark Twain Prize?

The playwright George Bernard Shaw once said that Mark Twain taught him "telling the truth is the funniest joke in the world."

With that in mind—and to paraphrase Huck one more time—this book was made by Mr. Cappy McGarr, and he tells the truth. Mainly.

TWAIN PRIZE WINNERS ON THE TWAIN PRIZE

No matter how serious the occasion, if you give comedians the opportunity, most will use it to make a joke. The following are the reactions of every Mark Twain Prize recipient when they have been selected for the honor.

1998: Richard Pryor
"I feel great about accepting this prize. It is nice to be regarded on par with a great white man—now that's funny! Seriously, though, two things people throughout history have had in common are hatred and humor. I am proud that, like Mark Twain, I have been able to use humor to lessen people's hatred!"

1999: Jonathan Winters
When asked by PBS what being awarded a prize in Mark Twain's name meant to him, Winters said, "I think I always dreamed—certainly as a young boy, maybe I do now, still—of standing on the banks of the Mississippi, and seeing this great-looking man with snow white hair. It's Mark Twain, and he's looking out at a whale boat…and Huck Finn over here, and I'm Tom Sawyer."

2000: Carl Reiner
In an interview with the *Washington Post*, Reiner said being selected was "kind of shocking. I didn't expect people would think about me like that…I think comedy always reflects the

times. Comedians don't move the times, but they are the first to notice it and point it out."

2001: Whoopi Goldberg

"Our dear Mister Twain put it best when he said, 'Humor is the good natured side of a truth.' I am deeply honored to join the ranks of Carl Reiner, Jonathan Winters, and Richard Pryor, who, along with the great Samuel Clemens, are some of the most fabulous truth-tellers of our time."

2002: Bob Newhart

Bob joked to the *Washington Post* that receiving the award was so unbelievable that the moment they handed it to him he would wake up next to Suzanne Pleshette and say: "Honey, I just had a dream you wouldn't believe. I just dreamed I won the Mark Twain Award!"

2003: Lily Tomlin

"I am truly honored to be recognized in the name of Mark Twain, an American humorist who was beloved throughout his lifetime and beyond, even as he imparted a strong and vital social consciousness that still resonates today. And I am truly humbled to be mentioned in the same breath as the great humorists of our culture, the past winners of the Mark Twain Award—Richard Pryor, Jonathan Winters, Carl Reiner, Whoopi Goldberg, and Bob Newhart. Thank you for the privilege of being in their company."

2004: Lorne Michaels

At the ceremony, Michaels said: "Other than the fact that I work or have worked with some of the best comedy writers of my time, I couldn't think of any reason I should be receiving this award. And then I thought of *Huckleberry Finn*, which I read as a boy and as a young man, and again a few years ago. And I realized that *Saturday Night Live* has always been stuck in adolescence. That time of life when you first begin to question your authority, declare your independence—a time of risk and adventure, and occasional bad behavior."

2005: Steve Martin
"I think Mark Twain is a great guy, and I can't wait to meet him."

2006: Neil Simon
"I am awed, thrilled, and delighted to receive the Kennedy Center Mark Twain Prize...it makes up for my losing the Samuel Clemens Prize."

2007: Billy Crystal
"To be given the same award as Richard Pryor, Steve Martin, and Neil Simon is a great honor. As my grandfather said, 'If you hang around the store long enough, once in a while they'll give you something!' I told my granddaughter, who is three, that I won the Mark Twain Prize, and she said 'I have one too.' I'm looking forward to a wonderful evening."

2008: George Carlin
"Thank you, Mister Twain. Have your people call my people."

2009: Bill Cosby (rescinded in 2018)
"After bathing us, dressing us in fresh pajamas, and setting us into the crib together, Annie Pearl Cosby read to my brother James and me *The Adventures of Tom Sawyer*, and later *The Adventures of Huckleberry Finn*. I would like to apologize to

Mister Twain for falling asleep hundreds of times, but he should understand that I was only four."

2010: Tina Fey
"I am truly thrilled to receive this honor. I assume Betty White was disqualified for steroid use."

2011: Will Ferrell
"I am truly honored to receive this distinction. I will now begin cultivating a Mark Twain-esque moustache in anticipation of the event."

2012: Ellen DeGeneres
"It's such an honor to receive the Mark Twain Prize. To get the same award that has been given to people like…Tina Fey and Will Ferrell, it really makes me wonder…why didn't I get this sooner?"

2013: Carol Burnett
"I can't believe I'm getting a humor prize from the Kennedy Center. It's almost impossible to be funnier than the people in Washington."

2014: Jay Leno
"What an honor! I'm a big fan of Mark Twain's. In fact, *A Tale of Two Cities* is one of my favorite books!"

2015: Eddie Murphy
"I am deeply honored to receive this recognition from the Kennedy Center and to join the distinguished list of past recipients of this award."

2016: Bill Murray

"I'm honored by this award and by its timing. I believe Mark Twain has rolled over in his grave so much for so long, that this news won't disturb his peace."

2017: David Letterman

"This is an exciting honor. For thirty-three years, there was no better guest, no greater friend of the show, than Mark Twain. The guy could really tell a story."

2018: Julia Louis-Dreyfus

"Merely to join the list of distinguished recipients of this award would be honor enough, but, as a student of both American history and literature, the fact that Mister Twain himself will be presenting the award to me in person is particularly gratifying."

2019: Dave Chappelle

"I did not write a speech."

PREAMBLE

When I began telling people that I was writing a book about my life and the Mark Twain Prize for American Humor, there's one question I got more than any other:

"Do you have any *other* book recommendations?"

The second question was usually: "Why?"

Not too long ago, a rabbi friend of mine shared some wisdom from the Talmud: to live a full life, a man must plant a tree, have a child, and write a book.

Having metaphorically planted trees in finance, and having raised my children, I was inspired by his quote to complete the set—and thereby live a Talmudically full life.

So I dug deep into my memories, and have conjured up stories from throughout my life—from my formative days at the University of Texas, to Goldman Sachs, to building lifelong friendships with national politicians, to getting appointed to the board of the Kennedy Center by two different presidents, to the creation and execution of the Mark Twain Prize—I've met a ton of wonderful people, and I'm going to tell you about them all here.

Still, it's a careful balance to strike. I've read books from self-important business figures, and they come off like an excuse to list off the celebrities they've met and fund a couple Lamborghinis.

I have no intention of doing that. Sure, I could brag about the relationships I've developed over the years with political titans such as Lloyd Bentsen, Tom Daschle, Al Gore, Bill Clinton, and Barack Obama. But that would be gauche.

I could regale you with all the times I rubbed elbows with entertainment stars—the likes of Tina Fey, Bill Murray, Eddie Murphy, Mel Brooks, Aretha Franklin, and Paul McCartney. But I would hate to name-drop.

Plus, I would feel remiss if I bought a luxury vehicle in this day and age and didn't go American. So, no Lamborghinis.

In all seriousness, I realize any memoir requires some delusions of grandeur from its author. But, as best as I can, I've tried not to make this book about me. Instead, it's about the value humor can bring to politics and life in general—the way differences can be bridged by a funny story or a silly impression. There's a joy shared when comedians make politicians laugh, and vice versa.

The way I see it, in Washington, there aren't enough funny people, and too many jokes. So I do my damnedest to bring that lighthearted, humorous approach to my family, and to Washington. That's why the Mark Twain Prize is so important. It's an annual reprieve in the nation's capital from the severity of the news—a chance to celebrate people who keep our spirits up in the face of challenges. And an opportunity to remind our leaders not to take themselves too seriously.

The journey to make the Mark Twain Prize happen has been quite a ride, and it's come with its fair share of surprises—none more shocking than when that same rabbi friend called me to sheepishly admit that he had discovered that the quote that he shared with me wasn't from the Talmud at all. It was *schmegegge*, which is Yiddish for *malarkey*, which is Biden for *bullshit*.

But it was too late: I had already started to write my book. And if that isn't funny, I don't know what is.

Steve Martin, Jimmy Kimmel, Martin Short, Bill Murray, and Cappy McGarr.

Tom Daschle, Bill Clinton, and Cappy McGarr.

INTRODUCTION

Delirious in the Oval Office

It takes a lot for the people who work in the West Wing of the White House to be starstruck. After all, these folks toil in the inner sanctum of the highest office of the most powerful country in the world—they're meant to be unflappable. It would be unseemly if, every time some figure of note showed up for a meeting, they became a bunch of lookie-loos jumping over each other to say hello, shake hands, and take a photo.

But when Eddie Murphy visited the White House, that's exactly what happened.

In the fall of 2015, Eddie was being recognized with the Mark Twain Prize at the Kennedy Center in Washington, DC. It's an award that celebrates those who have contributed to American humor at a level comparable to the achievements of Mark Twain. (As you can see, I'm on a first-name basis with Eddie. I know him as Eddie, and he knows me as a guy who calls him Eddie.)

As a member of the Kennedy Center's board of trustees, I helped create the Mark Twain Prize in 1998. And every year since, I've had the privilege of assisting in the selection process, gathering speakers to pay tribute to the nominee, and putting together an evening that combines the prestige of the Kennedy Center with the loose atmosphere of a comedy show. Each recipient of the prize has broken barriers in comedy and inspired the generations that followed. They've brought joy to millions upon millions; their work has demonstrated an enduring influence on the industry and culture at large; they have proven that their talents extend far beyond any one joke or character. They are—to distill it to five words—really, really, really, funny people.

Eddie Murphy was, by any measure, an outstanding honoree—he is really, really, really funny, both on stage and in person. He was also surprisingly humble, and he couldn't have been kinder throughout the celebration.

Part of the custom of the Twain Prize is that whoever is selected receives an invitation to visit the White House and meet the president. Many accept; a few don't. As you might imagine, it depends on the president.[1] With Barack Obama in office, Eddie accepted the invitation.

It was a meeting of two giants, men who broke through societal barriers to reach the top of their respective professions.

Oh, and I was there too—along with Deborah Rutter, the president of the Kennedy Center. In fact, I organized the meeting. (That's something I've learned over the years about accruing influence and meeting powerful people: if you book the room, you usually get to attend the event.)

I started the custom of bringing the Twain honoree to visit the Oval Office with President Clinton in the late 1990s, and it continued with Presidents George W. Bush and Obama. The meeting is always an honor for the Twain Prize recipient and their guests. But this year in particular, there was a palpable electricity to the summit. You could tell that Barack[2] was genuinely a fan of Eddie, and vice versa.

---

1   Taft, for example, never held such meetings. Some might argue that's because the Twain Prize hadn't been invented yet, but I think it's because the guy had no sense of humor.

2   Or, as people who know him like I do call him: "Mr. President."

They had a great conversation. The president recalled watching Eddie Murphy's stand-up specials, *Delirious* and *Raw*, and confidently claimed he could quote both of them verbatim. (Remembering the raunchy content of those specials, I did not ask the president to prove it.)

Usually, during meetings like this, the president is the one being asked most of the questions. But this time, there seemed to be a pressing query on the president's mind. "Eddie, you and I are the same age." Eddie nodded. The president continued, "You have no gray hair. I got a lot of gray hair." He strung these facts together as if to ask, "What gives?"

"Well, Mister President," Eddie said, "you have a more stressful job than I do. You're president of the United States—the most powerful man in the world. I just make people laugh."

That's when Barack Obama looked in my direction, and asked me one of his trademark tough questions: "I'm funny, aren't I, Cappy?"

Out of the three of us, I was *clearly* the authority on comedy in the room. I'm no expert on the niceties and decorum of the Oval Office, but I do know this: when the President of the United States looks you dead in the eyes and asks you if he's funny, there's only one thing *to* say. It's the phrase everyone knows, whether you're a military commander receiving an order or a talk show host being asked whether you've really read *The Audacity of Hope*.

"Of course, Mister President."

Thankfully, in this case, I didn't have to lie—Barack Obama really is as hilarious as he is charming. Whether delivering a moving speech or telling a joke, he has always had a fantastic sense of timing.

From there, with the president's blessing, Eddie and I went into the Situation Room. That's where we encountered rows of high-level government officials—we're talking Department of Defense, Homeland Security, the CIA, the FBI, the National Security Council, and probably a few agencies we're not even allowed to know exist.

Most of the people in the room were pretty young, but they were all serious professionals, made to look even more serious because the whole thing (appropriately) resembled a government command center, like the ones you see on TV or in a movie. If I had to describe the tone of that room in one word, "giddy" wouldn't come to mind. But I'll be damned if every last kid in there didn't scramble to get their picture taken with Eddie Murphy. (Though since we were in the Situation Room, it was an orderly scramble.)

The White House was also generous enough to arrange a tour for Eddie and his family that same afternoon. There was a brief snafu when we realized Eddie's mother, Lillian, didn't have a government-issued photo ID with her, but that was quickly resolved when she found an expired credit card with her photo on it. (The White House has a rule requiring all visitors to produce a proper photo ID. Eddie Murphy has a rule that he doesn't tour the White House without his mother.)

As we walked through the Cross Hall in the White House, we encountered Everett Raymond Kinstler's presidential portrait of Ronald Reagan. I was standing behind Eddie as he took it in. Against my better judgment, I decided this would be a good time for me to bust out my Reagan impression. "Well, Eddie, welcome to the White House," I said in Reagan's trademark raspy whisper.

Eddie liked it enough to ask me if I had any others. Soon, we were exchanging Jimmy Carter impressions, and then I broke out my closer: Bill Clinton, at the height of the 2016 campaign, revealing just how efficient a leader he really is; "Well, uh, I hope Hillary wins. I'll be interviewing interns two at a time."

At the rehearsal dinner the following evening—which I emcee every year before the actual Mark Twain Prize ceremony—we were treated to some really hilarious toasts from Arsenio Hall, Trevor Noah, and Dave Chappelle, among others. Eventually, I called Eddie Murphy up to the stage, which led to the scariest moment of my intermittent comedy career. Eddie leaned into the microphone, and said "Cappy is so funny…he does impressions." He shot me a look as if to say, "I'm about to tell you to get up on this stage and make a fool of yourself, and there's nothing you can do about it."

My emotions went from flattered to terrified. This was a dinner with Kennedy Center bigwigs, professional comedians, members of Congress, and VIPs of all stripes. It was *not* the ideal venue to try out untested comedic material.

"I'm going to go back to my table," Eddie said. "Call me back up using your Ronald Reagan voice."

I desperately didn't want to, but as with an invitation from the president, you can't turn down a call from Eddie Murphy to do your act. With no other choice, I took the mic, looked out at the crowd, and channeled my best Reagan:

"Well, Mommy and I," I said, "when we were in the White House, we traded places just like you did in that movie. And so, well, Eddie, come on up."

Later, Eddie signed my poster commemorating that year's ceremony with the ultimate validation: "Cappy—you should be doing stand-up!"

At moments like these, imposter syndrome kicks in, and you realize how challenging it can be to keep one's cool when shaking hands with the president or trying to get a laugh from a comedy all-star. Every once in a while, I can't help but ask myself: How the hell did I end up here?

This book is the answer to that question.

Cappy McGarr and Eddie Murphy at the Mark Twain Prize rehearsal dinner.

Cappy McGarr and Eddie Murphy with the bust of Mark Twain in the Rose Garden at the White House.

CHAPTER ONE

Everybody Ready, Except Cappy

I was born at the Shannon Medical Center in San Angelo, Texas, a town which is the self-proclaimed sheep capital of the world (don't tell New Zealand). San Angelo has historically been a significant center for wool in the United States, and they even held an annual "Miss Wool of America Pageant" for twenty years—until it was put out to pasture.

My father, Ray, had a master's degree in drama from the University of Colorado. He and his best buddy, Fess Parker, had appeared in some plays together and decided to try to make it as actors in Hollywood. So, my family moved to Los Angeles when I was just one year old. My grandfather had pursued a more traditional Texan career—he was in the oil business—so he gave my father an ultimatum. "You've got one year to make it," he said, "and if you don't, you're going to come back to work for me and be a roughneck."

As it turned out, my dad and Fess would both become roughnecks of sorts. My dad ended up going back home to work on oil rigs, and Fess Parker—yes, *that* Fess Parker—played Davy Crockett in the 1950s Disney miniseries.

We ended up moving from town to town throughout Texas, wherever my grandfather was drilling a well—from Eagle Pass to Sterling City to Coleman back to San Angelo.

Speaking of my lineage, let's play a game of "spot the mistake" with my patriline:

Wilbur Howell McGarr (my grandfather)

Wilbur Ray McGarr II (my father)

Wilbur Cappy McGarr III (me)

What the hell happened here? There's no Wilbur Ray McGarr I, and no Wilbur Cappy McGarr I or II—and yet, my dad's and my existence would heavily imply that's the case. Luckily my mother, Carolyn, helped put an end to the madness. She hated the name "Wilbur," which may have had something to do with the fact that she was none too fond of Grandfather Wilbur. So, by the time she enrolled me in grade school, I was Cappy Ray McGarr, the first and only.

I never knew any differently. It wasn't until college that I realized the name "Wilbur" was on my birth certificate, and then I decided to legally change my name to Cappy Ray. (So there you have it—you can put the Cappy McBirther movement to rest.)

Humor was a huge part of my life growing up. Like so many people, my first foray in trying to make people laugh took place at the dinner table. It was great to have an audience. Sure, it was just my parents, my sister Marla, and my brother Casey—but an audience of four isn't bad for your early routines.

Away from the dinner table I was trying to be funny too. In sixth grade, my teacher, Mrs. Howell, became acutely aware that I was a terrible speller. (The original title of this book was *The Mahn Hoo Meyd Merk Twaim Famiss.*) Accordingly, she did what any responsible educator would do: she aggressively made fun of an eleven-year-old. Every time she mentioned an upcoming spelling test, she would get in a little dig at me: "I'm sure everyone will do a very good job, except Cappy," she'd say. It genuinely hurt my feelings; I was so embarrassed.

I would have written her an angry letter, but it would have been completely illegible.

At one point, I ran home and cried to my grandmother—bless her heart, she did everything she could to help me memorize my spelling words. But it didn't make me any less upset. I had to do something to redress the ill behavior of Mrs. Howell. So I resorted to humor, or what I thought was humor. The next time Mrs. Howell made her snide remark—"everybody ready, except Cappy?"—I responded with, "Mrs. Howell, if I make a one hundred, will you kiss my heinie?"

You would have thought the comment might have earned *me* the Mark Twain Prize. Alas, all I got was an express ticket to the principal's office. As I awaited my fate, my mother was brought in to school too, and as we sat outside that office, she asked me what had happened. I obviously didn't feel comfortable repeating the joke to her, so I just said, "I got in trouble." But she pressed, so I repeated it. Ever the supportive parent, mother burst out laughing, but she quickly said, "You *are* in trouble."

My punishment was to take a walk around the school during every single recess for the rest of the year. The unintended side effect was that some kids viewed this as a martyr's victory lap, because they hated Mrs. Howell just as much as I did.

Comedy helped me find my place in the world too. When you're a kid moving from town to town, you gotta make a quick impression on people to make friends. And on the mean streets (or dirt roads) of rural Texas, that means being tough or funny. (I'm not ashamed to admit that I was only one of 'em—and it wasn't tough.) If you can make tough friends who think you're funny, you can reap both benefits. This was true when it came to the biggest kid in the class, Richard.

One day I strode right up to him. "Richard," I said, "I get into a lot of fights…"

"Yeah, I know," he said, looking confused. "You get your ass beat."

"...so you and I need to be best friends," I said, ignoring the truth about my ass.

But if he became my best friend, I wouldn't get my ass beat anymore—that logic was good enough for me, and for him too. We indeed became best friends, and my ass-beatings receded.

Years later, I was in the office of my frat in college, when a guy told me someone from San Angelo was there to see me. It was Richard. We hadn't spoken in years, but we caught up like no time had passed. By then, he was this huge offshore rig worker—the roughneck I never became.

It was a good lesson to learn early: get on the good side of the most powerful guy in the room. (You see how this thinking applies to fundraising for senators.) Over the years, I've found that making someone laugh is one of the easiest ways to break the ice and begin a friendship.

CHAPTER TWO

Apparently Fairly Bright

"Cappy is boyishly handsome and apparently fairly bright."
—The Rag

I am a proud alumnus of the University of Texas. It's where I jump-started my career and met lifelong friends and colleagues. What made me choose Texas? There was one reason, above all else: I got in. I applied to two colleges: UT and Georgetown. The biggest difference between them, for my money at least, is that Georgetown rejected me, and UT did not.

My grades in high school had been pretty average, and UT accepted me only on the condition that I would start pursuing my degree that same summer. I'm not sure if that was meant to be a deterrent—given Austin's sweltering heat, and students' aversion to summer school—but I took the deal.

Pretty soon I joined a fraternity, and while I was "merely a spectator" at some of its wild, debauched parties—not to mention hootenannies and shindigs—I was its treasurer, and then its president.

It was during this period of my life that I first began to realize I had a knack for raising money. As president—much like many people in Congress today—a huge part of my job was running around the state begging people for cash.

Admittedly, these were small-scale fundraising efforts. We'd need $200 for rush or $250 to repair a leak in the ceiling, and I would ask alumni for as little as $5, or maybe $25 tops. (All I'm saying is, the Democratic Party would be proud of young Cappy's ability to solicit small-dollar donations.) As I got more involved in the fraternity, I started to have more influence at the university as a whole, to the point that one of my friends, Sandy Gottesman, asked me to help him with his campaign for student body vice president.

Sandy was an almost-perfect young politician—tall, handsome, popular—but like a lot of politicians, he ran into trouble when he opened his mouth. He didn't say anything controversial; he just couldn't enunciate to save his life. He came from mumble beginnings; originally from New Orleans, he talked like his mouth was stuffed with shrimp jambalaya.

Our mutual friend and Sandy's campaign manager, Gary Kusin, asked me to go on the stump with Sandy at all the sorority houses to help him make his case. I would give impassioned speeches— throwing in the occasional joke too—all the while clamoring about all the fantastic things that Sandy was planning to do for the UT community. Sandy's only job, meanwhile, would be to stand there, be good-looking, and say "Thank you very much."

And it worked—he won. (It was basically the Reagan playbook.) It was fun to run around and advocate on behalf of a candidate like Sandy, and it certainly wouldn't be the last time I did such a job. But after that experience, the next year I decided to make a go for the VP slot myself. This was 1973—right after *Roe v. Wade*—and the cornerstone of my platform was an effort to get abortion access in the student health care center. As you might expect, this was a contentious position, especially in Texas almost fifty years ago. (To give you an idea about how liberal an idea this was, students at UC Berkeley were still campaigning to implement abortion access on their campus in 2018.)

It just felt like the right thing to do. It certainly earned me my detractors, but it also got me support from true believers. That's the trade-off—when you go out on a limb, you're operating on the hope that the people who defend you will be as passionate as the people who attack you.

Luckily for me, that's what happened. I got a call from a guy named Steve Gutow, a UT student and community organizer, who had heard about my candidacy. He told me he could help me get an endorsement from *The Rag*, an underground student newspaper. I visited the newspaper with him, and I got the endorsement. It was a proud moment, which was not at all diminished by the fact that it read: "Cappy is boyishly handsome and apparently fairly bright." Really, I love that. It strikes the perfect balance between a proper endorsement and damning with faint praise. Especially since they felt the need to use *two* qualifiers: "apparently" and "fairly." I had it framed and put it in my office. It was apparently fairly an honor.

Between the endorsement, the platform I ran on, and the Greek system behind me, I won the election. This meant that I would get paid $350 a month during my tenure as student body vice president, which was great until I realized that the president got $400 a month. I should have run for president.

Unfortunately, because it was a controversial proposal and subject to relentless university bureaucracy, we weren't able to fulfill our pledge to get abortion access in the student health center. It was my first time dealing with a politician who overpromises without understanding the limits to what is possible, though it would be the last time that politician was me.

It didn't take long for "the press" to turn against me. While I was serving as VP, the university's flagship newspaper, *The Daily Texan*, published a letter asking: "Has there ever been a more ineffectual bootlicker ever to attend the University of Texas than Cappy McGarr?" I knew the editor of the paper, so I called him up and asked him why the hell they would publish such a letter—he admitted they published it because they thought it was hilarious.

In fairness, I thought it was hilarious too, and like the "apparently" and "fairly" thing, I had the letter framed. I always think it's important for people to have a sense of humor about themselves—whether they're the president of the United States or a scrappy young kid working in student government—because it communicates humility and an ability to find common ground with the people you're serving, even if the common ground you find is to agree that "this politician is a jackass."

That being said, one thing I *am* proud that we accomplished was establishing a day care center on campus for students and faculty. So, take that, *Daily Texan*. I was apparently a fairly *effectual* bootlicker after all.

CHAPTER THREE

As Goober Goes, So Goes the Station

In addition to the lavish $350 per month that came with being student body vice president, I had to put myself through college with other odd jobs—the silliest of which ended up being the most rewarding.

As a one-off, I recorded a PSA for that year's Silver Spurs Rodeo, an annual fundraiser raising money for children with disabilities. I did the spot in character, doing my best Jimmy Stewart impression. (By the way, the key to a good Jimmy Stewart impression is to talk in a raspy voice, then pause, stutter, and, uh, p-p-pause again.)

As a result, I got a call from David Jarrett, who was a disc jockey for the 6:00 a.m. to 9:00 a.m. morning program at KNOW. He loved the ad, and he asked me to come into the station to do voiceover for some more promotions. So, I went in and did my impressions of Jimmy Stewart, Lyndon Johnson, Clark Gable, and Cary Grant, and he offered me a paid position as his sidekick on the show. Since I'm not one to turn down money to hear myself speak, I accepted and started going in to prerecord segments three times a week.

I jumped into the show with the attitude that it would be a fun little side project, and while it started out as just a harmless series of japes, in some ways what we did actually took on more significance than we originally anticipated. As just one example, I created a character named Goober Hoedecker, whose voice was a cross between Lyndon Johnson and a country bumpkin. (Yes, there is a difference.) His backstory was that he owned a "horny toad ranch" in La Grange—a nod to the Chicken Ranch whorehouse that Dolph Briscoe shut down—and that was basically all there was to him.

Goober was the id of the show, meaning Goober could say things that David and I couldn't necessarily get away with. One memorable example of Goober's hijinks came on the day before Richard Nixon's resignation. As Goober, I called the White House press office demanding to speak to Nixon's press secretary, Ron Nessen. They kept asking who Goober was, and whether he had credentials, and Goober kept repeating, "This is Goober Hoedecker from KNOW News," and insisting to speak with Nessen.

Sure enough, Nessen got on the phone. Knowing we only had a few seconds of his attention, Goober got straight to the hard-hitting question: Would Nixon resign? Nessen immediately hung up, but it was more than enough material for us to throw on the air the next morning and laugh about it. With that kind of stunt, we found ourselves reaching a sizable audience; in fact, the morning program on KNOW had the highest ratings in the Austin area. That, in turn, gave us leverage to properly execute one of our most ambitious premises: Goober running for mayor.

To be clear, the Hoedecker campaign was purely satirical. I wish I hadn't had to spell that out, but such subtleties were somehow lost on some of our listeners. For example, Goober claimed to come into work every day by landing a Learjet on Nineteenth Street (what is now Martin Luther King Jr. Boulevard in Austin). We actually got actual calls from actual people who were disappointed that they'd woken up at five in the morning only for no landing to materialize.

Goober was a single-issue candidate. His platform, as he described on-air, consisted solely of "getting elected officials on KNOW in order to ask them ridiculous questions." And that's exactly what we did. As Goober, I recorded silly interviews with every member of the city council. At the time, I was working as an aide to one of the city council members, so access wasn't terribly difficult. After that, I just had to make sure that none of the interviewees had the good sense to hang up once they heard Goober's goofy voice.

Mostly, the questions focused on how each council member was planning to work with Goober after inauguration day. In other words: they were inane, absurd, unproductive conversations. Accordingly, we had a fantastic time.

The truth is, these interviews were mutually beneficial. By getting guests who possessed some level of power, we were keeping the program relevant and exciting. And for a city council member, it's tough to say no to free publicity on the city's most popular radio show. Plus, any politician gets brownie points if they seem to have a sense of humor about themselves, even if they're faking it.

Our "Goober in Conversation" series culminated with the mayor himself. Roy Butler was running for reelection unopposed—with the exception, of course, of Goober's insurgent campaign—and getting him on the line was our biggest coup of all. Of course, I took the opportunity to be as much of a smart-ass with him as possible.

As he did with everyone, Goober deliberately got the mayor's name wrong, just to get him riled up. Then Goober made sure to ask "Mayor Cutler" about the most pressing thing facing Austinites, at least as far as Goober was concerned: "Mister Mayor, the big issue of the day is these massage parlors that have been popping up around town." (Let's be clear: there are massage parlors, and then there are "massage parlors." Goober was referring to the latter.)

Goober continued: "Opponents are trying to keep them outta certain neighborhoods with zoning ordinances, so I have to ask—"

I could already feel the mayor's trepidation as he asked through gritted teeth: "Yes, Goober?"

"Mister Mayor, have you ever been to one?"

Silence. Then, more silence. Eventually, the mayor gave what I thought was a surprisingly composed response: "No, Goober. You'll find out when you become mayor that you won't have time to go to a 'massage parlor.'"

The interview quickly ended after that, but by our criteria, it had been a resounding success. Imagine our horror, then, when the station manager burst into the control room moments later, in a frenzy: "The mayor just called me. He's furious and does not want that interview to be aired on KNOW in the morning. He is absolutely forbidding it."

To me, even though this was hijinks, being banned by a politician was devastating—and unacceptable. It was the closest I have ever felt to being an intrepid journalist, forced to choose between protecting my career and upholding the truth. Except instead of upholding the truth, I was trying to uphold my right to ask the mayor obnoxious questions.

David and I genuinely believed that the interview was defensible and that it would be beneficial for the station if we broadcast it. We played the tape for our manager, and thankfully, he thought it was hilarious too, so against our collective better judgment, we let it air the next morning.

It just so happened that the KNOW morning time slot ended around the same time I started my shift as a city council aide, meaning that day, I essentially entered the belly of the beast directly after the interview aired. I had made some effort to keep Goober's identity anonymous, but Mike Levy, who had just founded *Texas Monthly*, had blown my cover in the magazine's gossip column. In the fleeting moments I had alone with my thoughts as I approached the building, I considered whether I should have perhaps maintained a more professional distance from Mr. Goober Hoedecker.

I arrived at the chamber, and as was my luck, one of the first people I saw was Mayor Butler. Thankfully, he wasn't able to confront me immediately, because he was surrounded by people fawning over how funny his appearance had been, and what a great sport he had been for doing it.

With newfound confidence, I approached the mayor and asked him how he was doing. And without even a hint of amusement, Mayor Butler said: "McGarr, strike one."

I'm still not sure why the mayor took it so seriously—clearly, Goober was the only one coming out of that exchange who looked foolish. Also, I'm not sure what kind of retribution the mayor was planning to enact against me if I got to strike three. It's just as well that I never found out.

I can hardly claim that Goober's antics on the radio were a heroic case of a comedian speaking truth to power, but, during my stint at KNOW, I got to experience firsthand the way that comedy can bridge gaps—in this case, between the college student who isn't engaged in local politics and the elected official who might have forgotten how to get a message across to regular people.

That's what the best comedians do. In making us laugh, they make us consider new ideas. In pointing out the hypocrisy of our leaders, they invite us to critically look at the world. And in releasing tension, they provide catharsis during challenging times—both personal and political.

And yet, for all the positive impact they can have on society, I've always felt that comedians haven't received the kind of cultural reverence that Americans offer to other artists.

Sure, individual work has been recognized—there's the Grammy Award for Best Comedy Album, and the Emmy for Outstanding Comedy Series. But those are ultimately subcategories in institutions meant to honor television and recording—the comedy aspect is a sideshow. And the Academy Awards are infamous for snubbing comedies. Comedians host the show, but rarely are comedies recognized as the art they are. (In nearly a century of ceremonies, comedies, which represent about a third of all movies released, have received only a handful of Best Picture wins.)

I always felt comedy deserved respect as its own genre. And I felt that my comedic heroes should be acknowledged for their entire body of work, which can span from movies and television to albums and live performance. (And shouldn't there be a ceremony to honor them that, in and of itself, is funny as hell?) Decades down the line, these would become some of the fundamental ideas that would guide the creation of the Mark Twain Prize.

No matter the medium, no matter how mainstream—from the most popular *Tonight Show* segment to the forgotten broadcasts of Goober Hoedecker—comedy's core has stayed the same: it's a genre with an edge, a safe haven for weirdos and outcasts, and an outlet for the little people to crack wise at the powerful. And for most of its history, it has been woefully unrecognized for the joy it consistently brings people. I may have quit comedy after college, but I've never quit my efforts to pay tribute to the comedians who have inspired me then, before, and since.

CHAPTER FOUR

Blind Leading the Blind

It was both an honor and a little terrifying to have started a feud, however in jest, with the mayor of Austin. And I had a great time messing around on the radio with all the city council members and then seeing them the next day at work. But I never would have had the chance to build those kinds of relationships without the mentorship of one (until now) unsung public servant, and a man who would come to be hugely important in my life.

In my early college days, I was raising money for my fraternity, working my way through our alumni lists to find potential donors. I didn't recognize the name Lowell Lebermann, but as he was on the list I went to pitch him at his office.

Mr. Lebermann was a distinguished-looking guy, especially as he had a patch over his right eye. In that first meeting, I'd arrived with a couple of financial needs. In addition to our typical rush fundraising, we'd had to borrow $250 from Frank Denius, our chapter advisor, so that we could fix a leak in our roof. I decided to leave that part out—I didn't want Lebermann to get bogged down in the details—and besides: I never raised more than $25 at a time anyway.

When Mr. Lebermann asked me how much money I was looking to raise, I just told him that we were looking to get a few dollars here and there for rush. His response caught me off-guard: "McGarr, that's bullshit. I already know you need two-fifty to fix the leak in your roof."

Evidently, he had already been in contact with Frank. I stammered: "Sir, that's true. But I also need money for rush, because it's coming up and we've borrowed some money already—"

Graciously, Lowell Lebermann didn't let me ramble any further. Instead, he waved over his assistant to bring him a check, already made out for $300—$250 to fix the leak and $50 for rush. He carefully placed his hand on the check and handed it in my direction, but I noticed that his uncovered eye seemed to be staring right through me. And that was the moment that I realized Lowell was completely blind. (He'd lost his vision in a gunshot accident, but he retained motor control over his left eye—so he could always have his eye on you, even without being able to see.)

Three hundred dollars was the largest gift I had received from any individual by then, and as time has passed, I've learned that *all* politics is transactional, on some level. If you notice someone being suspiciously generous with their time or money, there may well be some kind of quid pro quo involved.

And so it was: as he passed me the check, Lebermann said: "McGarr, this is a bribe."

Turns out he wanted our fraternity to get involved in his city council campaign. Some of us would work directly for his campaign; others would boost turnout and support from students.

At the time, I was still running to be vice president of UT's student body, but I told Mr. Lebermann that after the election, I could turn over my campaign infrastructure to him. My campaign infrastructure, of course, was composed of the services of my two buddies. I may not have had PAC money, but I did have Tommy Graves and James Little. They would go on to work on Lowell Lebermann's campaign, while I served out my term as student body VP. And after I completed my term, Lebermann hired me as his aide in city council.

I had visited his office hoping to get, at most, $25. Instead, I got $300 and my first job out of college. It was the best (and, I'll clarify for legal reasons, only) bribe I ever accepted. Plus, this started a tradition of Lowell hiring all his aides from the frat house, which lasted for the rest of his career.

I had arrived at UT pursuing a BA in government, but my term as student body vice president had extended past when I was scheduled to complete that degree, so I added a journalism degree too. Then I went to work for Lowell, while still raising hell over at the radio show.

I kind of got to have it both ways. I was goofing around and making fun of people in power, while having the privilege of working with them in a serious capacity. In fact, I may have loved it too much. The radio show was performing greatly, I was fresh out of college, and I had a hearty dose of Texas-sized confidence. For a fleeting moment, I considered a big leap: moving to Los Angeles and pursuing a career as a stand-up comic. It would have brought me full circle: I could have given myself the same one-year deadline that my dad had to become a professional actor.

But Lebermann brought me down to earth, urging me instead to pursue a business degree when I finished at the city council. He didn't tell me I *couldn't* give LA a shot, but he said if I did, I would "probably be dead in a ditch in two or three years from a drug overdose." Statistically—we're talking about the stand-up comedy scene in the 1970s here—he probably wasn't far off.

During my time as Lowell's aide, I was constantly by his side. Every day, I would read him the paper and go through his mail. At the city council chamber, I had a microphone with a direct link to Lowell's earpiece that I used to brief him on the council agenda and his talking points. Later, I would guide Lowell through functions with his constituents, giving him directions. "The podium where you're speaking is at three o'clock; the gentleman you're paying tribute to is ninety degrees to your left; the donor who won't leave you alone is directly in front of you, approaching fast."

Aides to politicians are often considered to be the eyes and ears of the operation. In my case, I was *literally* seeing for Lowell. In turn, I got to learn just as much about disability advocacy in helping him navigate the world as I did about Austin, local government, and public service.

I ended up working for Lowell for a year before taking his advice and pursuing my MBA. For decades, we maintained a close friendship. We took trips together, I emceed his big birthday celebrations, and he even became godfather to my daughter Kathryn. It became difficult to remember a time in my life where he wasn't just a phone call away.

Lowell liked to say I never stopped working for him, because I would always take his calls. I don't know where I would be if he hadn't taken a chance on me. Perhaps more than anyone else in that time period, Lowell helped me to figure out a plan for my life—or maybe I should say a direction. Because I've never been the type of guy to craft a master plan for what I want my world to look like years in advance. Life just doesn't work that way. But it helps to pick a direction. Lowell helped me to see things more clearly. And yes, I am aware of the irony in that.

On July 9, 2009, Lowell passed away in Aspen, Colorado, at the age of seventy. A memorial service was held a week later in the auditorium of the LBJ Library at the University of Texas at Austin. That space fits about a thousand people, and it was filled to the brim, which just goes to show how important Lowell was to so many people in Texas, right up until the end of his life.

Virginia Lebermann, Lowell's daughter, asked me to give a eulogy for Lowell that day. I told stories about so many of the laughs we shared over the years, from dinner chats to birthday roasts. At the end, I quoted the line from "Amazing Grace" that summed up his impact on me:

"I once was lost but now am found,
Was blind, but now I see."

After delivering the eulogy, I arranged for an African American choir to sing "Amazing Grace." There wasn't a dry eye in the auditorium—including mine.

CHAPTER FIVE

An Unidentified Aide

J 've been fortunate to meet and work with multiple United States presidents between my time as a political fundraiser and board member for the Kennedy Center. But my first professional encounter with a president happened when I was twenty-one years old.

At UT, I studied under Professor Elspeth Rostow, a legend on campus who would go on to become the dean of the LBJ School of Public Affairs. She had worked for the Office of Strategic Services in Washington during World War II, and married Walt Whitman Rostow, who served as a key national security advisor for Presidents Kennedy and Johnson. From the first moment of her first class, we realized she was an extraordinary woman and teacher. She had an impeccable sense of fashion, too—and not just by academic standards. Eventually she became my faculty mentor and advisor for a three-hour-per-week course on President Johnson.

I idolized Johnson and still do. Between Medicare, Medicaid, the Civil Rights Act of 1964, the Voting Rights Act, the establishment of the Corporation for Public Broadcasting, the National Endowment for the Arts, the National Endowment for the Humanities, and on and on, his domestic achievements were second only to Franklin Roosevelt's, and his civil rights achievements were second only to

Abraham Lincoln's (understanding, of course, that the shadow of Vietnam still looms over his legacy).

Professor Rostow and I met in the fall of 1972, and as we moved toward the end of the semester, I began to wonder what my final exam would look like. But whenever I would ask Professor Rostow, she would demur and simply say she was thinking about it.

Soon enough, I got a call from a guy named Bill Wright, President Johnson's administrative assistant. He said, "Get your only suit on and meet me at the LBJ library tomorrow afternoon at three o'clock. You've got a meeting with me, Elspeth Rostow, and Harry Middleton." (At the time, Harry Middleton was the director of the LBJ Presidential Library, and before that he had served as one of Johnson's speechwriters and staff assistants.)

The next day, I put on that one suit (as Bill correctly guessed) and walked over to the LBJ Library, where Harry Middleton said, "Cappy, we would like for you to be the president and Mrs. Johnson's aide during the upcoming Civil Rights Symposium."

The Civil Rights Symposium was an event being held at the library that December, and President Johnson was set to give remarks. I was awestruck, but before I could get a big head, Middleton said, "This is the job: If President Johnson wants a cup of coffee, go get a cup of coffee. If Lady Bird needs you to run downstairs and get somebody, run downstairs and get somebody."

Then came the kicker. "Elspeth tells me that you've been studying President Johnson for the semester. This job is going to be your final exam, and you're going to be getting your grade from President Johnson. Don't think it's going to be easy; he's a very tough grader." I looked at Mrs. Rostow, who just smiled.

I was probably the most excited any student had ever been to take a final exam.

When the first day of the symposium came, it felt like everyone in President Johnson's orbit was there: Andrew Young, the civil rights activist and an executive director of the Southern Christian Leadership Conference; Earl Warren, who served as chief justice of the Supreme Court during Johnson's term; and Hubert Humphrey, who served as Johnson's vice president.

The only person missing was the president. He was set to arrive in grand fashion: flying in on a helicopter from his ranch in the Texas Hill Country about sixty miles away and landing on a helipad on top of the library. That helipad was built specifically for Johnson, and him alone. After he passed away, the FAA determined it was too unsafe for use. (Library staffers later used the deck to sunbathe.)

The problem was, that day it was sleeting in Austin. And just like when it rains in Los Angeles or hails in Atlanta, everyone was freaking out—the president would have to be driven into town.

Mrs. Johnson was in the green room with the president's doctor, on the phone, trying to convince her husband not to make the trip in the inclement weather. He had been having heart issues, and they were begging him to wait until the weather was clear to make his way over.

Undeterred, President Johnson had the Secret Service put chains on his tires; apparently he got so frustrated by how cautious his driver was being that he took over. Once he'd arrived, in the green room one of his people introduced him to me. Any president is a powerful presence by the mere nature of the office, but at 6'4", and strutting around the presidential library named in his honor, Johnson was especially intimidating. His greeting to me was brief.

"I understand you're my aide," he said, but before I could even finish nodding, he began barking orders. "Now, go get my speech! I want it on five-by-seven cards. Liz Carpenter has it upstairs."

Liz Carpenter had been an aide to the Johnsons for over a decade. She had been LBJ's executive assistant while he was vice president and served as Mrs. Johnson's press secretary during Johnson's presidency—I had met her while working as Lowell Lebermann's aide. In the moment, though, her most important title was "the lady I gotta get the speech from."

I managed to sputter out the words "yes, sir" before I zoomed up the elevator to the eighth floor to find her—she handed me a pile of papers and said, "Here's the speech. I don't have it on five-by-seven cards."

I returned, terrified of delivering bad news to a president on my very first assignment. My hand shook as I handed him the speech, and just as I feared, he said, "I thought I told you five-by-seven cards!" When I told him that Liz Carpenter hadn't offered the speech on cards, Johnson said, "Did she give you any grief?" Again, before I could even compose a reply, he let out a big, hearty laugh and said, "Don't take any guff from Liz Carpenter."

Then, things took a turn for the bizarre: When it came time to head to lunch, President Johnson dispatched me to locate Hubert Humphrey, who had evidently been sick with a stomach virus. I went over to the green room bathrooms, and after calling, "Mister Vice President?" a couple of times, I finally got a response from behind the door: "Yes, yes, I'm here!"

I let Mr. Humphrey know the president was waiting for him. Mr. Humphrey let me know that he was going to take as long as he was going to take. I tried not to think too much about the fact that I was a twenty-one-year-old kid trying to rush an ill former vice president off the toilet. Thankfully, he eventually exited of his own accord, and the festivities continued as planned.

The following day, as Earl Warren was giving the keynote speech for the symposium, I was seated next to the former president and Mrs. Johnson, and a UPI photographer snapped our photo. The next day, to my surprise, I woke up to a bunch of phone calls from friends around the country—apparently, the photo had appeared in newspapers from Washington to Dallas and everywhere in between. In the *Houston Chronicle* the photo ran on the front page. I was elated, until I read the caption: "President Lyndon B. Johnson, Lady Bird Johnson, and an unidentified aide." (I would come to find out later that only the *Chronicle* bothered to *un*identify me.)

The symposium concluded with remarks from President Johnson. I got to witness them from the front row, sitting next to Mrs. Johnson. The president's doctor had warned him not to exert his limited energy by speaking for too long (in fact, to mitigate his chest pain, he was popping nitroglycerin pills during the speech), but the former president had too much to say.

On the role of government in achieving equality: "I believe that the essence of government lies with unceasing concern for the welfare and dignity and decency and innate integrity of life for every individual...regardless of color, creed, ancestry, sex, or age."

On voter participation: "I have no doubt but what this would be a better country and a purer democracy if ninety-five percent of our people voted and the five percent that didn't had an exemption because of illness or whatever it might be."

On the work left to be done: "To be Black in a White society is not to stand on level and equal ground. While the races may stand side-by-side, Whites stand on history's mountain and Blacks stand in history's hollow. And until we overcome unequal history, we cannot overcome unequal opportunity."

All told, he spoke for about half an hour. For a man of his health, that was a formidable effort. Afterward, a member of CORE (the Congress of Racial Equality, the civil rights group) began shouting at Johnson. Before anyone could silence him, the president said, "Let the man speak," and gave him a platform to talk about all the ways that Black Americans still experienced inequality.

When he'd finished, Johnson came back in front of the podium, said the protestor was right, and went on to speak with conviction about the steps that would need to be taken to end inequality once and for all. It was a classy move. At the end of his big speech at his own presidential library, Johnson had the humility to share the spotlight for the greater cause.

As for that grade? I got an A. I was never the type of student to brag, but I'm proud of that one.

✦　✦　✦

Not long after, once finals had been completed, and I was headed back home to Dallas, Bill Wright called me to say that the president had a gift for me. I couldn't get back to Austin until the next day, but Bill told me not to worry about it, that we would reconvene when I came back to school the next semester.

Bill never got back to me. Not long after I came back to Austin in January 1973, Lyndon B. Johnson died. His remarks at the symposium would be his final public speech before his death.

Later on, when I was vice president of the student body, I got a call from Lady Bird Johnson's assistant, saying that Mrs. Johnson, who was on the UT Board of Regents at the time, wanted to have lunch with me. I thought the meeting was going to be about some university issue, but as we sat down for lunch, she took out a photograph and handed it to me. "The president ordered this," she said. "He wanted me to give it to you and thank you for being our aide."

It was a print of the photograph of the three of us, and one of the very last photos of the president before he died. I couldn't believe it. I was overcome with emotion and gratitude. The fact that the president had it printed, and that Mrs. Johnson was thoughtful enough to make sure I received it after his passing, is one of the greatest honors of my life. And best of all, there is no caption labeling me as an unidentified aide. Instead, it read: "To Cappy, on a day to remember, Lady Bird Johnson."

I have now served on the LBJ Foundation for over twenty years, where I've had the privilege of continuing to work with the Johnson family and their associates. It's an honor to play even a small role in upholding the legacy of the single most effective president of my lifetime.

President Lyndon B. Johnson, Lady Bird Johnson, and an unidentified aide.

Stonewall, Texas

September 5, 1990

Dear Cappy,

These days I almost never come to the office. As a matter of fact I'm 'closing up shop' and retiring from just about everything except for the LBJ Library and my own 'forever' project, the National Wildflower Research Center.

While I'm happy to cast aside duties and obligations, it's letters like your's that made coming to work a pleasure. And your kindness gave me a shot of adrenalin on a busy day. The Civil Rights Symposium stands out so vividly from those last years of Lyndon's life -- a sweet and moving testament to what he believed in and tried to do. I'm deeply touched it will always stay a part of your memories, too.

Thank you for your thoughtful words and photograph, which I treasure having.

With much affection to you and Janey,

Lady Bird

CHAPTER SIX

The Soufflé Never Rises

*G*etting the chance to serve as President Johnson's aide was a humbling experience for me, but there was one connection I made through student government that was even more transformative.

As vice president of UT's student body, I was given jurisdiction over half of the appointments to the boards and committees we oversaw. And because there was no rule against it, I gave myself the best position: a spot on the union board. That got me access to free movie tickets, concert tickets, and bowling passes. Discounts tend to corrupt, but free stuff corrupts absolutely.

That's where I met Janie Strauss. She was the head of the Union Program committee, and she was looking to run for chair of the board in the fall after returning from summer break. I was all for Janie—poised, whip-smart, kind—becoming chair in the fall, and I decided I wanted to serve as chair over the summer. In addition to the perks that came with being a member of the board, being chair got you a stipend of $325 a month. Combine that with the $350 a month I was getting from being VP, and I could basically become the John D. Rockefeller of 1970s college students. I was on the fast track to becoming a junk food *tycoon*.

So I sought to strike a deal with Janie: if she would back me as chair for the summer, she would have my full support when the fall semester came around. Janie agreed to my plan; I got my summer stipend, and in return, I rigged the vote to ensure Janie got elected unanimously to be chairman during the school year. (The French call this a *coup d'é-Cappy.*)

The next day, I asked her out on a date. I figured that if I could convince her to go with my cockamamie board-succession plan, maybe getting dinner wouldn't be too much of a stretch.

We immediately hit it off. She was smarter, kinder, and (frankly) better-looking than I was. The one thing I had going for me is that she would laugh at my jokes. If you don't think I'm funny, you also have to give Janie credit for her patience and acting ability.

My favorite movie is *Casablanca.* Early in our relationship, there was an auditorium presenting a special one-night-only screening of the film. We waited in line, excited to watch *Casablanca* on the big screen together, until we got to the front and found out it was completely sold out. Why didn't we reserve tickets earlier that day? "I never make plans that far ahead."

I was really disappointed. It may seem small, but that didn't make the pain any less real.

A few months later, our first Valentine's Day together truly cemented our relationship. Janie had spent the previous summer at a cooking school in the south of France, and she told me she was going to cook us a soufflé at her apartment. My only job was not to be late, because, as they say, a soufflé only rises once.

I was late. On my way over, I stopped at the first payphone I could find, rushed on the line to let her know, and sped my way to her place.

There was no soufflé. What Janie surprised me with was even better: she had set up an honest-to-God movie-theater-style projector, and rented, on film, reel-to-reel, a movie for us to watch while we had dinner. It was *Casablanca.* Complete with the hot dogs, cherry sours, and Dr. Pepper we always got from the concession stand.

I mean, come on. How could I not want to marry the woman who put that together? People spend their whole lives looking for "the one." If you ask me, the definition of true love is the thoughtfulness and care it took for Janie to re-create the perfect evening we thought we had lost—no soufflé necessary. As it turns out, I've still never seen Janie make a soufflé.

We continued to date as I finished school, worked at the city council, and got my MBA. Eventually, I proposed, in as straightforward a way as possible: after one of our dates, I simply gave her a call, and asked her point-blank if she would marry me. She said, "Yes, but why don't you come over and ask me again in person and we can discuss it."

We got married in Janie's backyard on May 27, 1978. Janie had contracted bronchitis a couple of days beforehand, and after the ceremony, it only got worse. The honeymoon was a disaster: Our first port of call, Palm Springs, California, featured unbearable 115-degree weather, so we decamped to Disneyland, where we got stuck on the "It's a Small World" ride and were forced to listen to the theme song for forty-five minutes straight. Then Janie got bronchitis; we ended up in Big Sur, specifically The Big Sur *Lodge,* run by the KOA, rather than the superior Big Sur Inn—our hack travel agent hadn't seemed to understand the difference. But we survived it all, and we've been able to laugh together about that catastrophic week for the last forty-three years.

After marrying Janie, I met two of my most dedicated and influential collaborators: our daughters, Elizabeth and Kathryn McGarr.

Close to midnight at Presbyterian Hospital Dallas on July 15, 1982, Elizabeth Nan McGarr was born. It was one of the most wonderful moments of my life. From the first moment I held her in my arms, she looked up at me with the big, curious, expressive eyes that I still see today.

Our second daughter, Kathryn Jane McGarr, was born on June 3, 1985, at that same hospital. One of the first things she did in her life was to sleep on my shoulder. It was our second go-around, but when she was born, I was once again completely floored by the joy and love and excitement that came from introducing a child to the world.

Elizabeth grew up to become the senior editor of *Sports Illustrated* in charge of *SI Kids* until late 2019. She is the one person I know who had a specific professional dream at the age of eleven and actually fulfilled it. Now she is a full-time mother. Meanwhile, Kathryn has written a book with another one on the way, she's won awards, and now she's an accomplished professor at the University of Wisconsin. I couldn't be happier for and prouder of the both of them.

CHAPTER SEVEN

The Goldman Age

Once I'd gotten my MBA, it was time to find a job, but I had procrastinated setting up interviews. The dean of the business school, George Kozmetsky, pulled some strings for me so that I could meet with Goldman Sachs—I was squeezed into the very last spot on their schedule.

I met with a guy named Pete Coneway (he would eventually become the ambassador to Switzerland and Liechtenstein under President George W. Bush). Coneway was tan, had perfectly groomed blond hair, and wore a coat that had buttons all the way to his elbow. He just exuded money—and the most important question he asked me was a simple one.

"Why do you want to work for Goldman Sachs?"

I said, "Because you guys pay the highest starting salary." That got a laugh out of Coneway, so I didn't let on that I was being serious.

Something about my chutzpah, I guess, made him like me (plus, like me, he'd once been the president of his fraternity and VP of his student body, so we were basically the same person, minus the money). He sent me to interview in New York, where a guy named Bill Gruver asked me if I'd read the *Wall Street Journal* that day.

I had skimmed it, sure, and told him so.

"You *glanced* at it?" Gruver snarled. "You must not be right for Goldman Sachs if you just *glanced* at it. We want people who *read* it."

Oops.

"Did you read it front to back or back to front?"

Like just about everyone, I tend to read things front to back, but apparently that was wrong too. "Goldman Sachs likes people who read it *back to front* because all the investment articles are in the back," he said, as though I was a toddler being toilet trained.

I left convinced that the interview had gone so terribly that I would have to write off Goldman Sachs altogether and start the job search anew. I was ready to write my own obituary—back to front, of course. But apparently Goldman Sachs must have decided that if I could handle forty-five minutes in a room with Bill Gruver, I was ready for the rigors of the financial industry.

✦　✦　✦

After completing my MBA, I moved up to New York and started Goldman's training program. As soon as I arrived, we were introduced to our two training supervisors: Roy Zuckerberg and the one and only Bill Gruver.

One day around lunch, not long into the training period, I got a call from Gruver, who sternly asked me, "Henry Fowler wants to see you. Do you know why?"

At the time, Henry Fowler was a partner at Goldman Sachs, but he was better known as the former secretary of the treasury under President Johnson. I knew enough to understand that he's a guy you either *really* want to call you into a meeting or *really* don't.

What could I possibly have messed up this early in the process? I felt like I was being called to the principal's office, times one thousand. (And this is coming from an *expert* at getting called to the principal's office.)

The elevator zoomed up to a floor too high for me to count. The doors opened to the partners' dining room, and there I was, a trainee entering the power center of the operation. Soon enough, I found Secretary Henry Fowler. As I carefully approached, he revealed why I was there: "Cappy, Lady Bird called me. She said I should get to know you and have lunch with you."

It was a fantastic lunch—he welcomed me to the company, let me know that he had heard nothing but kind words about me, and encouraged me to reach out to him if I ever needed anything. And it was all thanks to Lady Bird Johnson, who had already given me so much before I even graduated from college. Once again, I was humbled beyond measure.

When I came back downstairs, Gruver demanded to know why I had been called for that meeting, so I gave him a taste of his own medicine. In as terse and matter-of-fact a tone as I could muster, I simply said, "Bill, it was a nice lunch…and a *private* conversation."

✦ ✦ ✦

After the training period, I came back down to work in the Dallas office and stay close to Janie. A few years into working there came one of the most pivotal deals of my life.

My father-in-law had a buddy named Chuck Kuhn—he was the guy who lent his place in Palm Springs for Janie's and my honeymoon—and he let me know that he was planning a merger for his company, Wylain, Inc. At Goldman Sachs, if you brought in a piece of corporate finance, you would receive a small percentage of the fee that the company received. Chuck knew this and was hoping to help me score that check.

Accordingly, I went to the top partner in the Dallas office, Tommy Walker, and connected him with Chuck. A few months went by, and Chuck called me to tell me that I was about to get a nice payday. My finder's fee was supposed to be in the neighborhood of $45,000.

(This was strikingly similar to the $40,000 in student loans I was trying to pay off.)

Right after I got that call, I went to Mr. Walker, and I asked him exactly how much of the fee I was supposed to be getting for the deal. He looked perplexed. The deal had been months in the making, and he didn't remember I had brought it in. He called in the VP who had overseen the merger, and she claimed that she had no idea I was even involved, which was a load of BS. (Baloney Sachs.)

I wasn't just a part of this deal; I was the only reason it was happening. With my anger up, I made it clear that I knew Chuck Kuhn very well, and I could call the deal off with a single phone call. If I wasn't getting paid, none of us were. (I should note I had confirmed this plan with Chuck beforehand.) Big surprise, the deal closed, and I got paid. The day the check cleared I paid off my student loans, and the next day, I quit Goldman Sachs.

Stuff like this can happen all the time in corporate finance, so you have to be aggressive. (Later on, when I started my hedge fund, Goldman Sachs would be my prime broker, and in that respect they were always the best people to work with.) Aggressive or not, I had unemployed myself at thirty-three years old. But I knew how to raise money, make connections, and close deals. By leaving Goldman Sachs, I was giving myself the opportunity to see if I could cut out the middleman and forge a path of my own.

CHAPTER EIGHT

Senator, You're No Lloyd Bentsen

*B*y the time I quit Goldman Sachs, I knew a few key things about myself: I was invested in politics, I was good at raising money, and I loved making people laugh. In a perfect world, I could find a passion that would bridge those three areas as much as possible.

As it turns out, hosting fundraisers for Democratic candidates fit the bill. I've had the privilege of raising money on behalf of some of the most honorable politicians (not an oxymoron!) of the last few decades. And the best part is, when people come to you looking for money, they're *much* more likely to laugh at your jokes.

Unless their name is Lloyd Bentsen.

By the time I started paying close attention to politics, Lloyd Bentsen had already served his country longer than I had been alive. He was in the Air Force during World War II, got elected to the US House of Representatives in 1948 and served through the mid-1950s, and in 1970 he defeated George H. W. Bush to become the junior senator from the state of Texas. He ended up winning reelection by a huge margin in 1976.

When Senator Bentsen's reelection came around again in 1982, an aide to Bentsen named Jack Martin asked me if I wanted to help the campaign. By that time, between student government elections, fraternity fundraising, and working for Councilman Lebermann, I had gotten pretty good at getting people to open their wallets. So another Bentsen supporter, Pete Geren, charged me with co-chairing a Young Persons for Bentsen committee—called the Committee of 50—along with Scott Atlas. Scott would become a prominent Houston lawyer; Pete would become a congressman and Secretary of the Army under Presidents George W. Bush and Barack Obama. We were the original Dream Team, if you swap athletic ability for the skill of courting donors. (Actually, Pete played varsity football for Georgia Tech, so I guess he can have it all.)

Throughout the campaign, we organized fundraisers, made phone calls, twisted arms—whatever it took to load up Senator Bentsen's war chest. But the most memorable event from that cycle came after Bentsen won reelection, and it put me face-to-face with the man himself.

Ann Richards was the governor of Texas at the time, so we got to hold a "thank you" reception at the Governor's Mansion with a bunch of important Texas people, including Senator Bentsen and, of course, Governor Richards. We had cocktails inside the mansion, and there was a big tent set up in the front for dinner.

I emceed the event, which was a lot of pressure, considering the audience. Ann Richards was famous for her sharp and unsparing wit—she famously said George H. W. Bush was "born with a silver foot in his mouth."

She always used her wit as a sharp political tool, so trying to be clever in front of her would be like performing a cello recital in front of Yo-Yo Ma. Fortunately, the night went off without a hitch. Afterwards, we were all hanging around—Senator Bentsen, Governor Richards, the fundraising committee folks, and me—and Senator Bentsen told me something I was not expecting to hear: "Cappy, I understand you do a great impression of me."

"Senator, I have no idea what you're talking about," I lied.

But it was too late. The other guys from the committee were egging me on too. Lloyd's wife, B. A. Bentsen, said she wanted to hear it too. Evidently, everyone but me was already in on this. Then Ann Richards chimed in: "I've heard you do Lloyd Bentsen, and you need to let him hear it right now." Given her tough demeanor, it was already hard enough to say no to Ann Richards, but in Texas? While she was governor? At a Democratic fundraiser? In her *mansion*? It was basically an executive order.

So I had no choice—I mustered up my best refined, soporific drawl, and said, "This is Lloyd Bentsen, man of the people. I wear Hermès ties, and I'm the senator from France."

The impression got a good laugh from everyone there, with the notable exception of its inspiration. Senator Bentsen was stone-faced. He just looked at me and said, "Well, that's the last time you're going to do an impression of me. I can assure you of that."

I'll admit it may seem like a fairly gentle comeback on paper, but when Lloyd Bentsen sizes you up and cuts you down, he gives off such an air of gravitas and dignity that it makes everything he says hit hard. (I can't imagine how Dan Quayle must have felt after their VP debate.)

✦ ✦ ✦

His unhappiness with me didn't last long. Over the years, he and I became friends, and I continued to work with him for many years. He would go on to become chair of the Senate Finance Committee, be nominated as Michael Dukakis's running mate in 1988, and after Bill Clinton was elected president, Bentsen was selected to be the secretary of the Treasury.

As I started my hedge fund and sought investors, Lloyd Bentsen was even happy to be my reference. But in 1993, after Bentsen was tapped to lead the Treasury Department, Bob Strauss (Janie's uncle, and a close friend to Bentsen) gave me a call and told me I needed to take Secretary Bentsen off my reference list. Bob's reasoning was that it wouldn't look good for a Treasury secretary to have a money manager citing him as a reference.

"Bob," I said, "don't you think Bentsen would let me know if he wanted me to take him off my reference list?"

Bob gave it to me straight. "You dumb sonuvabitch, he's not gonna go out of his way to ask you that. Just call him and let him know you're taking his name off."

So the next time I was in Washington I called Bentsen. He was a busy guy, so we walked and talked in his office building. I told him what Bob had said. Secretary Bentsen smirked, and in his deadpan, asked: "Oh, so Bob Strauss is telling me what I should do now?"

"Let me tell you this," he went on as we strolled, "I *insist* you keep my name on your list as a reference. And I reserve the right to tell people *exactly* what I think of you." He smiled, I thanked him, he said, "You're welcome," and that was that.

Here's the thing: Bob hadn't been wrong—a truly careful politician probably would want to cut ties from any money managers after being nominated to run the Treasury Department. But Lloyd Bentsen put loyalty over optics. Even if it would have benefited him politically, he wasn't about to throw me under the bus. (That's the secretary of transportation's job.)

✦   ✦   ✦

There is obviously a transactional nature to the relationship between politicians and fundraisers, but there is also a difference between people who just call you up when they need something and partners who consistently check in and are invested in you as a person. Lloyd Bentsen was squarely in the latter category. And it's no coincidence that figures like him were, by far, the best people to raise money for.

The pitch for him was straightforward too: "He's a great guy, a dedicated public servant, a legend within the Democratic Party, and chairman of the Senate Finance Committee."

But he's the gold standard. I can't imagine how it must feel to raise money for certain people in Congress today: "He's a snake, he doesn't know anything, and no one likes him." Tough sell.

CHAPTER NINE

Landslide Daschle

By the mid-1980s, my hedge fund was in full swing, I had fund-raised for a bunch of election cycles, I was serving on the boards of the Dallas Symphony, the Dallas Assembly, and the Dallas Zoo, among others, and I had begun my lifetime appointment as father to Elizabeth and Kathryn McGarr. Suffice it to say, I was burning the wick at both ends and from the inside out.

That's when I got the call from Lloyd Bentsen. If the Democrats won the majority in the 1986 midterm election cycle, he was on tap to chair the Senate Finance Committee, and he wanted to know if I could do a fundraiser for a young congressman who was running for Senate. "I'm planning to put him on the finance committee if he wins," Bentsen said.

I had already done a bunch of political fundraisers and was totally burned out. Both my pockets and the pockets of my Dallas contacts had been vacuum dried by that point. But Bentsen wouldn't take no for an answer, so the young congressman came down to Dallas, and we threw him a fundraiser at our house. He was a kind, down-to-earth guy, who in all the best ways reminded me of a Boy Scout. He had served in the Air Force as an intelligence officer; then, he worked in the House on behalf of Vietnam veterans by passing legislation to research the health effects of exposure to Agent Orange. By any measure, he seemed like an upstanding fella.

His name was Tom Daschle.

Even though it was a relatively small event, we ended up raising somewhere in the neighborhood of $2,500, cobbled together in increments of a couple hundred bucks here and there. For a fraternity, that would have been a great haul, but for a candidate for the United States Senate, it was a drop in the bucket. Through it all, though, Representative Daschle was gracious and kind, and he won by about nine thousand votes. That may sound like a close election, but it wasn't by Tom's standards: when he was first elected to the House in 1978, he won by just 139 votes. From that point forward, he carried the nickname "Landslide Daschle."

Right after the election, Senator-elect Daschle asked if I would host a reception where he could thank everyone who had come to the initial fundraiser. This was unprecedented in my experience; I had never heard of a political candidate offering to come to an event for his donors with no presumption of fundraising. And since he was going to sit on the Senate Finance Committee, he would have even more influence; with that in mind, the ever-savvy Lloyd Bentsen suggested that we make the event a fundraiser anyway. Bentsen told me to call every lawyer at every law firm and every bank and everyone who donated to his campaign. I was to tell them that the newest member of the Finance Committee was coming down to Texas.

It's pretty unusual to get people excited about an election six years out; then again, it's unusual to get a show of goodwill from a politician like Daschle had offered. With the power of Senate Finance Chair Lloyd Bentsen pulling in Texas money, we raised around $75,000 for Tom Daschle's next Senate campaign.

By the time Tom ran for reelection in 1992, he and I had become close friends. It was a presidential election year, and that summer, the Texas billionaire Ross Perot was leading President George H. W. Bush and Governor Bill Clinton in the polls. I had already introduced Tom to Ross Perot and his son—who, as it happened, was also named

Ross Perot. Tom had helped Ross Perot Jr. secure funding for the Fort Worth Alliance Airport, and I had gotten Ross Jr. to do a fundraiser for Tom in Fort Worth. And although my radio days had long since ended, I never stopped working on my impressions—including one of Ross Perot Sr.

Just for fun, I rang Rita Lewis, Daschle's finance aide, and I tested my Ross Perot out on her. Once I heard her cackle and snort over the phone, I knew she would be game to help me pull off a little prank on Tom. She called Nancy Erikson, Daschle's office gatekeeper who would later go on to be Secretary of the Senate, and asked her to tell Tom that Ross Perot was on the phone.

Daschle picked up a phone in his gentle, unassuming tone: "Ross, how are you doing?"

"Tom, this country's in serious trouble," I jibber-jabbered.

"Well, I've seen the way you've traveled around this country and discussed the issues affecting America, and I've found it all very impressive," Tom said, ever the diplomat.

"Tom, the real reason I like you is that you're short, just like I am." I was pushing my luck now.

If I had been impersonating any other politician, this line would have been a dead giveaway. But hearing a bizarre statement like that from Perot wouldn't have been out of the ordinary. Daschle chuckled a bit, and said, "Well, Ross, you've got a great sense of humor. Let me tell *you* a joke."

As he started to tell the joke, I realized something: Tom was seriously buying the impression, which was both flattering for me and terrifying for our national security. For the sake of everyone involved, I needed to nip this in the bud right then and there. Halfway through, I broke character and interrupted him: "Tom, Tom—"

"Ross, Ross, I'm here."

"Tom—it's Cappy."

Silence. Then, without a hint he was remotely amused, he asked, "Is anyone else on the phone?"

I admitted that Rita Lewis was on the phone too, at which point she burst out laughing. I took the chance to throw her under the bus, falsely assuring Tom that she *made* me impersonate Perot. "I did not!" she shouted, in between snorts and giggles. Still nothing but silence from Daschle. Eventually, he said: "This better not be in *Roll Call* [the Capitol Hill gossip mag]. I've got to go."

The next morning, I was having breakfast with Jack Martin, who was still working for Senator Bentsen, and I just had to tell him the whole story. I implored him not to tell anyone else…at which point he immediately told Senator Bentsen. Bentsen, in turn, relayed it to a group of lawmakers in the Senate cloakroom, who buckled over with laughter. That's when Daschle himself entered the cloakroom, and Bentsen had to regain his composure to greet him.

From my understanding, this is how the interaction went down:

"Tom," the Texas senator said, "I understand that a constituent of mine called you yesterday."

"Is that so?" Daschle responded, completely oblivious. "Well, who might that be?"

"I understand it was Ross Perot. I understand that he called you a midget and asked you to be his running mate."

I had no idea all this had happened until my secretary came through the door and said, "Cappy, Senator Daschle's on the phone."

He let me have it.

"Does the word 'discreet' have any meaning to you at all?[3] I can't walk the halls of Congress without someone saying, 'Hey, Daschle, how's Perot doing?'"

---

3   From *Merriam-Webster*: "having or showing discernment or good judgment in conduct and especially in speech." See also: refraining from blabbing about how you duped a senator to your buddies.

Ruffling Tom Daschle's feathers is something of an accomplishment—he's normally so composed; it's like trying to rile up the Queen's Guard outside Buckingham Palace. Eventually he came to see the humor in the whole thing, thank God. He would even end up telling the story at fundraisers as an icebreaker, proving that he does have a great *sense of humor*, even if it didn't always manifest in the form of well-delivered jokes. Let's be honest: there aren't a lot of people in his position who would have an ego restrained enough to take my little prank in stride that way—not to mention that he continued to take my calls.

Also, to be fair: Daschle's joke delivery improved dramatically over the years. In 2002, he delivered a humor routine at the Gridiron Dinner that is still thought to be one of the best ever.

His opening line brought the house down and made the *Washington Post*: "Hi. My name is Tom. And I'm an obstructionist. This is my first meeting. I haven't obstructed anything in the last twenty-four hours." That's just the kind of self-deprecating humor that defines the Gridiron Dinner, allowing politicians who are normally at each other's throats to laugh together and bond, even if just for an evening. (I take full credit as the guy who loosened him up.)

Tom eventually went on to become majority leader of the United States Senate, but he never lost that humble demeanor that he carried when I first met him as a representative. He's part of an endangered breed in politics: a true public servant with integrity, both in his ideology and his working relationships. If I could befriend any of 'em, I'd take Daschle in a landslide.

CHAPTER TEN

Follies, Legislative and Rabbinical

During the late 1970s, at the end of each Texas legislative session, a group of Austin political-types—mostly from the state legislature—would come together for a comedy show at Scholz Beer Garden called the Legislative Follies. It was a fun show to unwind at the end of each term that would include satirical songs and routines about the latest political developments.

The Legislative Follies, a recurring comedy show at Scholz Beer Garden in Austin, were an excellent opportunity at the end of each state legislative session for local politicians to poke fun at themselves and each other. Like any political satire, the Follies packaged important stories and issues in an entertaining, digestible way. You didn't have to be an expert on the legislative process to have a good time at the Legislative Follies—though it certainly helped to pick up on some of the in-jokes.

Ann Richards was performing in the 1975 edition of the Follies, and she gave me a call to recruit my talents: "Can you do a Dolph Briscoe?"

Dolph Briscoe was the governor of Texas at the time. He was most famous for closing the Chicken Ranch, which was an illegal brothel down in the Central Texas town of La Grange. This would inspire the musical *The Best Little Whorehouse in Texas,* which in my book is still the best musical about little whorehouses in Texas.

Briscoe was a conservative Democrat in every sense of the word, from his politics to his demeanor. The headline of his obituary in the *Austin American-Statesman* simply read, "Dolph Briscoe, a Texas ranch hand." And he had a Texas accent thicker than a double-meat Whataburger.

Point being, I could do a Dolph Briscoe.

Ann laid out the plan: We would perform as a duo, with myself as the governor and Ann as the first lady of Texas, Janey Briscoe. I was to show up in overalls, a cowboy hat, a work shirt, and blue jeans. For her part, Ann would wear a big black wig to properly capture the first lady's essence. Rumor was that in the Briscoe household, Janey Briscoe made all the real decisions, so in the skit, Ann would be delivering the thrust of the routine and my job was to respond—no matter what she said—with a big smile and declare, "Texas Today!" (Dolph Briscoe basically started every sentence that way.) Every time I yelled it, Ann would smack me in the back of the head and tell me to shut the hell up. It was broad, slapstick, and crude. And it totally worked.

Ann quit drinking in 1980 and began to identify as a recovering alcoholic. This incredible discipline guided Ann as she worked her way up to the Texas governorship, and she remained sober for the rest of her life. She never lost her cutting wit and willingness to have fun on stage. In fact, while she was still drinking, she told me that she was worried that she wouldn't be funny anymore if she stopped—but if anything, the clarity that came from her sobriety only made her funnier and sharper than ever. In later years, we would perform on the same lineup at all kinds of events, including a roast of Tom Daschle in South Dakota. But one show stands out that I was most proud to be a part of, and it was for my old friend Steve Gutow.

In the mid-1990s, after practicing law for over a decade, my dear friend Steve Gutow decided he wanted to become a rabbi. Coming out of the fourth year of his program, Steve and I got together for our annual lunch, and he gave me the update: for his fifth year, he would be studying abroad in Israel, and then he would come back to the United States to finish up his sixth and final year.

By that point, I had been a father for over a decade, so I was bursting with unsolicited life advice. I implored the rabbi-in-waiting: "Steve, you're almost fifty. While you're in Israel, you should find a nice Jewish girl, settle down and start a family."

"Cappy," he said, "you're probably one of the last people to know, I guess. I'm gay."

Before he even started rabbinical school, Steve had asked Ann Richards and me to perform at a roast for his graduation. When Steve's graduation finally rolled around, it was time to come up with some material. He assured me that any subject about his personal life was fair game, and that despite my ignorance of his sexuality, he had long since been out of the closet. I called up Larry Amoros, a friend of mine who *happened* to be Jewish, *happened* to be gay, and *happened* to be someone I could throw under the bus if the jokes didn't go well, and asked him to help. He was also a stand-up who had written for Arsenio Hall, would be one of the writers for the Mark Twain Prize ceremony, and in general was one of the funniest people I knew. He told me with genuine giddiness that he had been waiting his whole life to write gay rabbi jokes.

We worked together making the material just right. It had to be tasteful, but not too safe. It had to be provocative, but in a way that wouldn't get me in trouble. And it had to be funny enough to warm up the crowd, because I was opening the show. I don't care who you are. If you're on the bill with Ann Richards, she's the headliner.

The tribute was to be held in an auditorium outside a synagogue in Philadelphia. About five hundred people were gathered to honor Steve, which was intimidating, but I got up to the microphone and introduced myself, talked about how close I was with Steve, offhandedly mentioned that my wife was Jewish—getting all the credentials out there, just to be safe—and then, I brought up the conversation I had with Steve in which he told me he was gay.

You could have heard a pin drop. Clearly, the audience didn't think the subject was funny. So, I doubled down with the punchline: "Now, let's ask ourselves: What is a *shlomosexual*, anyway?"

The line got a huge laugh, and I could feel the crowd loosening up a bit. I hit them with my next zinger: "The real reason Steve wanted to become a rabbi was so that he could wear white after Labor Day." Given my lack of fashion knowledge, I actually didn't know *exactly* what that meant, but it worked.

Then I said: "Steve gave a sermon last Friday night and quoted this passage: 'And God said unto Moses: you look *fabulous!*'"

Finally, I pivoted to maybe the dumbest joke of them all. "Sue Fischlowitz is here. She's in charge of rituals at the St. Louis synagogue that Steve is moving to. What you might not know is she had to change her name because it sounded too Jewish. It was originally *Gefiltefischlowitz.*"

Any time you tell jokes in public, you've got to know your audience. And at a rabbinical school graduation celebration, using the word *Gefiltefischlowitz* is a pretty good bet. I told a bunch of other jokes in that fashion, and we had a great time. Once you get past the hurdle of making an audience laugh once, the rest is usually smooth sailing. Later on, of course, Ann Richards brought the house down with her infamous "turkey story" routine, in which she recounted how hunters like herself lured turkeys by imitating the mating calls of hens—and riling them up in the process. "There have been criticisms of people like us who enjoy going hunting. And I have tried to explain to them that never could any bird possibly meet their death in happier circumstances."

These days, Steve Gutow is one of the most influential rabbis in the country. Don't take it from me: *Newsweek* said so too in their annual listing of "America's Top 50 Rabbis."[4] He's taken the lead on a bunch of important issues, from fighting poverty to pushing for immigration reform to supporting the campaign to end gun violence.

The fact that, in spite of all the serious accomplishments he's had, he has always maintained such a great sense of humor about himself—it's as inspiring as anything else. I've already talked about how important it is for politicians to have a sense of humor, and arguably, it's even more important for faith leaders. The best religious communicators, like my friend Steve, have the humility to serve their communities over themselves. Bringing a bunch of friends together to joke about his life and identity was a sign that he was doing it right.

---

4   I've got as much of a shot of making that list as I do of getting "Sexiest Man Alive."

CHAPTER ELEVEN

Do It for Dallas

I've helped out a lot of candidates for a lot of elections on every level, from student government to the United States presidency. But one of the most exhilarating campaigns I've ever been a part of was actually the Dallas mayoral election of 1987.

Annette Strauss was running to be the first woman and the first Jewish person to be elected mayor of Dallas. And, as my wife Janie's mother, she would make history by being my first and only mother-in-law to be elected mayor.

Annette got elected to her city council seat in 1983 and was selected to be mayor pro tempore by her fellow councilmembers in 1984. By the time she announced her campaign in 1987, she had lived in the city for forty years and was a beloved member of the community, involved in everything from the arts to Planned Parenthood.

In Dallas, municipal elections are technically nonpartisan, which means there are no primaries, and no political parties listed on the ballot. Instead, all of the candidates compete in a single general election, and if no candidate gets more than 50 percent of the vote, the top two vote-getters advance to a runoff election.

With that in mind, Annette did very well in the general election; she got 43 percent of the vote in the first round, the highest percentage by far in the nine-candidate race. But because she didn't crack 50 percent of the vote, the election ended up going to a runoff between her and Fred Meyer, the former chair of Dallas Republican Party and a patrician Republican straight from central casting.

One of the most iconic moments of that campaign actually came out of an attack ad. The ad was just one example of a broader shift in Dallas politics that the election was reflecting; it featured a woman named Carole Young. Carole was a part of an organization called Leadership Dallas—Annette had done a fundraiser for Leadership Dallas at her home, and that was the one and only time she met Carole. Fred Meyer, on the other hand, was a good friend of Carole and her whole family. Nevertheless, the Meyer campaign built an ad around Carole's testimonial—"I know Annette Strauss," she claimed, "and she would be weak on crime."

Carole barely knew Annette—again, they met once—and Annette was pledging to hire 150 new police officers and was a longtime supporter of the Dallas Police Department. No matter—at the final one-on-one televised debate between Annette and Fred Meyer, my mother-in-law looked straight at the camera and said:

"You know, before I talk about the future of the city of Dallas, I want to say something about an ad my opponent is running, featuring a woman who claims to know me, saying I would be weak on crime. I wouldn't know her in a crowd of one. I met her once, in my home, and that was it."

Then she turned to Fred Meyer, shook her finger, and rebuked him: "Fred, you ought to be ashamed of yourself. You ought to be ashamed." Finally, she turned back to the camera, smiled wide, and moved on: "Now, let's talk about the future of Dallas."

It was the most poised, yet devastating set of opening remarks at a debate I'd ever seen. The blood drained from Fred Meyer's face, and he never recovered for the rest of the night.

This was classic Annette Strauss. She took her identity as a mother, and instead of letting it be used against her, she turned it around and made Fred Meyer look like an insolent child. Once the hit was complete, she pivoted to talk about the issues that mattered to the people of Dallas.

She won the runoff with 56 percent of the vote. And to her credit, Annette would become friends with Fred Meyer as she continued to work on behalf of the city of Dallas. There was no question that some Dallas landmark would have to be named after Annette.

✦ ✦ ✦

Annette's term as mayor coincided with the 150th anniversary of the city's founding in 1841, or the sesquicentennial.[5] To commemorate that occasion, Dallas was honored by a visit from Her Royal Majesty Queen Elizabeth II.

As mayor, my mother-in-law was tasked with selecting some children to give the visiting queen of England a bouquet of ceremonial flowers. As any loving grandmother would, she didn't hesitate to choose her granddaughters, Elizabeth and Kathryn. We ended up sending a great Christmas card that year with a photo from that day and the caption: "Happy Holidays from Elizabeth, Kathryn, and Elizabeth II."

The next most important ceremonial role in this whole charade? They needed the parents to stand behind the kids in case they freaked out. Janie and I were eminently qualified for that position.

Elizabeth McGarr I, who was ten at the time, had sewn an adorable dainty pillow (stuffed with cottonballs, and without any help!) as a gift. She even wrote a little tag to go with it: "To Queen Elizabeth, from Elizabeth McGarr." I took the chance to explain a gift my daughter was holding: "Your Majesty, my daughter is also named Elizabeth,

---

5   If you're wondering how to pronounce sesquicentennial, I say "150th anniversary."

and she has been sewing this pillow for you to keep on your bed at Buckingham Palace."

The queen turned it over, looked at it, smiled at her namesake, and said, "How lovely. It's absolutely wonderful in every single way."

Then the queen left with Annette and the two of them headed up the stairs of the Symphony Center. I stood with my daughter for a moment, and then she turned to me and said, "Daddy, she has an English accent."

"Yes, sweetheart. She's the queen of England."

Queen Elizabeth admires Elizabeth McGarr's pillow as the whole McGarr family observes.

Mayor Strauss would become so honored in Dallas that just before her passing they named a big outdoor performance venue after her called Strauss Square in a unanimous vote from the City Council.

There was no question that *some* Dallas landmark would have to be named after Annette, but it took some deliberation to land on Strauss Square. I had met with Ron Kirk, the mayor of Dallas at the time (and a future trade representative for the Obama administration), and I suggested that Dallas's Central Expressway be named after her.

Ever the observant politician, Ron shot back: "Are you kidding? People would be cursing her every time there was bumper-to-bumper traffic. 'I'm stuck on Strauss again!'"

Good rule of thumb: when it comes to public institutions, try to avoid being the namesake of highways, DMVs, and prisons. Ron was right, and he wisely suggested that her namesake be the venue in the heart of the Arts Center instead. It was just as well: her name deserved to be a destination, not the journey that made people run late to the destination.

Annette Strauss passed away in 1998 after developing a brain tumor. She was a force of nature right up to the end. She had the tenacity of a savvy dealmaker combined with the heart of a dedicated public servant. She lived by the creed that she would repeat anytime she was trying to solicit help from one of her many connections throughout the city: "Now, honey, do it for Dallas." I looked forward to her (frequent!) calls, when she would remind me, gently but firmly, "Honey, do this," or "Honey, do that." I miss those calls, and her, to this day.

My granddaughter is named in her honor: Annette Cap McCue. (I graciously accept the honorable mention in her middle name.) It's only a matter of time before little Annette starts calling me up and telling me what I oughta be doing too.

CHAPTER TWELVE

Waiting for Perot

*D*uring the 1988 presidential campaign, I was connected through Lloyd Bentsen with then-Senator Al Gore, who was making his first presidential run. I traveled with Gore as he made campaign stops around Texas in anticipation of Super Tuesday and cohosted a reception in Dallas to help him raise money. I've always liked working with Al. I admire his commitment to the environment, and he's easy to get along with.

Later on, in 1992, when President George H. W. Bush was running for reelection against Bill Clinton and Ross Perot—but before Gore made it onto Clinton's ticket—Gore was promoting his book *Earth in the Balance.* I invited him to speak about the environment to the Dallas Assembly (I was its president), an organization made up of young leaders from around the city across the worlds of business, charity, education, politics, and other industries.

On our way to the event, he asked me if I knew Ross Perot. At the time, Perot's campaign was surging—around then he was leading the pack with 39 percent of the vote, far ahead of both President Bush and Governor Clinton. His numbers made headlines in the *New York Times* and the *Washington Post*, and he even made the cover of *Time* magazine, with the caption: "He's leading in the polls, but can he lead the nation?" This was before he dropped out in July 1992 only to reenter the race in October, so he was still being taken seriously. Gore wanted to give Perot a copy of *Earth in the Balance* because he might end up being the president of the United States. (This was at a time when presidential candidates could be counted on to read books.)

I was able to coordinate the meeting with Perot, but first I half-jokingly asked Gore about his own presidential ambitions: "Al, why didn't you run this year? You're the exact opposite of Bill Clinton: You went to Vietnam, and he didn't. You smoked marijuana, and he didn't inhale." He chuckled a bit and was a good sport about it.

On the way to Perot's office, I told Gore the story about the time I prank called Tom Daschle as Ross Perot, complete with the catch-phrase "this country's in serious trouble." We waited for Perot in his office for about a half an hour, enjoying greatly how he'd decorated it: we sat in bright yellow chairs, and above his desk hung the original "The Spirit of '76" by Archibald M. Willard, the iconic portrait of Revolutionary patriots playing the fife and drum.

Perot finally arrived, and he was just as buoyant in person as he was on TV. The first words out of his mouth were, "This country's in serious trouble," but luckily we avoided cracking up into laughter, and Gore did manage to emphasize to him the importance of protecting the environment in the event that Perot became president.

Ultimately, Gore would become Bill Clinton's vice-presidential nominee and run on the ticket against Perot, but Perot continued to be politically active, running for president again in 1996. But there was more to him than the caricature—I saw him put in a lot of hard work to help the people around him.

During my mother-in-law's term as mayor of Dallas, any time a policeman got hurt or killed, Perot would anonymously set up educational funds for their families. Later on, in the early 2000s, when Tom Daschle was the Senate majority leader, I would get phone calls from Perot at all hours—we're talking 5:30 in the morning—because he found out about a serviceman overseas who needed medical treatment. Perot would use his plane to send a specialized doctor across the world, and he would ask me to get Daschle's help to expedite the doctor's visa or passport or whatever was necessary to get the job done.

✦ ✦ ✦

I didn't interact much with Gore after he ascended to the vice presidency. Toward the end of Clinton's second term, though, I got a call from Vice President Gore's office asking for a meeting. Accordingly I visited him at the vice president's residence at Number One Observatory Circle, shook his hand, and said hello: "Mister Vice President, great to see you."

He balked.

"No, no, no, Cappy. We know each other." And then, with seemingly no awareness of the Paul Simon song, he said, "You can call me Al." (They want you to know their first name when you sign the check!)

He asked me if he could count on my support when he ran for the presidency, and it was an immediate yes. He asked me if I thought Texas could be in play. I expressed my doubts about a Democrat winning Texas, but I also said: "You can raise a lot of money in Texas. But politics is all about reaching out, staying in touch, and telling people how much you love them. And the people I know in Texas have not heard from you."

The vice president said that he understood and asked me to get some numbers together for him to call personally. I gave him a list of fifteen or twenty Texas people who I thought could be really effective fundraisers for him, but in the end, he never called any of them.

Gore simply lacked the knack for retail politics that Bill Clinton, and later President Obama, would demonstrate. He was a little stiff, had trouble relaxing, and wasn't proactive in reaching out to people while he was serving as VP. Because of this, he developed a reputation of being boring and humorless—which anyone who knew him personally could tell you was far from the truth. But in a country where the charismatic, personable, funny candidate often emerges victorious, you can't keep that side of yourself private.

If he'd been better at wining, dining, wheeling, and dealing... maybe those 537 elderly Floridians who held the fate of the presidency in their veiny hands could have been brought around.

CHAPTER THIRTEEN

Crosby, Stills, Nash & Daschle

After serving in the Senate for nearly a decade, Tom was elected to be leader of the Senate Democrats in 1995. He held the role of minority leader from 1995 to 2001 and then presided as majority leader from 2001 to 2003. It would be a tumultuous two years in American history, encompassing the September 11 attacks, an anthrax threat against Daschle himself, the launch of the war in Afghanistan, and the buildup to the war in Iraq.

But in my view, the most controversial moment of Tom's career came when he aided and abetted me in committing a felony.

After Tom got reelected for a third term in 1998, I started and became the chairman of DASHPAC, which stood for the Dedicated Americans for the Senate and House Political Action Committee, named in honor of his father, Sebastian Daschle, a middle-class small-town guy who worked his whole life at an auto-parts company. He went by "Dash," and he had just passed away in 1997 at the age of eighty.

At one point, we gathered a group of donors to go out to South Dakota and spend some time with Tom in his home state, where we intended to scale the front of Mount Rushmore. Now, ordinarily, you can't just *do* that. The big appeal of this excursion was that, with Tom's authority, we could have an experience that was otherwise off-limits to the public.

At one point, I climbed on top of George Washington's big round granite head and heard a stern voice shouting from down below: "Sir, get down from there! You're committing a felony!"

It was the head of the National Park Service, whom Tom had invited to join us. He was literally the authority on the laws associated with national parks. We had to oblige, lest we get sent to park jail (or whatever power he had to punish us).

Soon thereafter, I got a photo in the mail—this fantastic picture of Tom and me posing at the bottom of George Washington's head. Tom signed the photo and left a note: "To Cappy, the only friend I've ever had who nearly got arrested on Mount Rushmore."

Cappy McGarr and Tom Daschle posing at Mount
Rushmore (with Lincoln just out of frame).

When I wasn't acting as Daschle's co-conspirator, I was organizing concerts to rally his donors. On one occasion we had David Crosby booked, and the comedian Lewis Black would open for him. I was aware that Black could be vulgar, and as the entire Democratic caucus was going to be in attendance—including a lot of senior senators who were old-fashioned—I wanted to warn him to be careful. Senator Robert Byrd was especially prudish, and I told Black that if Byrd heard the f-word even once he'd be highly offended (you would have thought that Byrd, a man who was once a member of the KKK in his youth, might not have taken a holier-than-thou stance on curse words, but who am I to judge?).

Lewis Black nodded and told me he understood. Then he got onstage, and the first words out of his mouth were:

"It's *f**king great* to f**king be f**king here in f**king *Washington, F**king DC.*"

Sure enough, Senator Byrd left the room, and I learned a valuable lesson: comedians value their free speech. If you say *nothing* to them in a sensitive situation, they *might* self-censor just because they think clean material will play better in an old-fashioned room. But if you draw a line and tell them they can't say something, suddenly their ethical code *behooves* them to break the rules. In other words: if you're worried they'll curse, telling a comedian not to do it is a self-fulfilling f**king prophecy.

David Crosby was another thing altogether. He did not include a single Crosby, Stills & Nash song in his performance—with the single exception of "Teach Your Children" at the very end—instead playing entirely new songs no one had heard of. Despite this, we still managed to raise a lot of money, but it was entirely because of the clout Tom had as the leader of the Senate Democrats. Senator Byrd ended up barging into Tom's office the next morning and chewing him out for the event's profanity. And Tom himself, whom you can usually count on to look on the bright side (if there is a bright side), admitted he didn't think it went well.

But we would get our redemption. In August 2000, we held a fundraiser in Los Angeles to coincide with the Democratic National Convention nominating the Gore-Lieberman ticket. We got Los Lobos to perform, and Stephen Stills as a guest singer. Los Lobos had gotten their start in Los Angeles, so they were playing on home turf and were sure to be a hit. Once Stephen jumped on stage with them, he knew how to please a crowd, and immediately broke out the classic "For What It's Worth." And they really milked it: everybody in the band took a solo, to the point that song alone became a full-blown concert experience that lasted almost an hour. It goes without saying that it brought the house down.

After the fundraiser was over, Tom and I went down to Stephen's green room to thank him. I said, "Stephen, we've had David Crosby; now we've had you. Do you think y'all could convince Nash to come to Washington so all of you could sing together at our next big fundraiser?"

"Anything for Senator Daschle," Stills said.

About six months later, DASHPAC's next fundraiser was coming up, and I had nailed down the entertainment. "You're not going to believe it," I told Tom, "I booked Crosby, Stills & Nash. It's going to be the biggest event we've ever hosted."

To which Tom said, "Cancel them. I don't want loud music. Harp music would be fine, but I don't want the loud music and a long evening." His argument was that people simply wanted to contribute, shake his hand, get a photo, and head home. (I also got the sense that he didn't want a repeat of the Crosby performance, which was fair enough.)

So that's what I did. As people came in the front door of the 701 Restaurant in Penn Quarter, where the fundraiser was being held, they were serenaded by a single harpist.

By the way—and this might seem surprising, given how many fundraisers I've hosted over the years—but I firmly believe we need to take money out of politics. It's not just that there isn't a level playing field; there is no playing field. Regular folks are left out of the process when politics comes down to who can court the richest donors. That's why I strongly support the public funding of elections. It would transform the whole electoral system in a way that brings power back to the people.

But until then, as long as other people are using their money to prop up blowhards, opportunists, demagogues, and ideologues, I see no issue with fighting back and raising cash for honest advocates who are dedicating their lives to uplifting underserved communities.

You gotta spend money to reduce the influence of money.

CHAPTER FOURTEEN

The Mark Twain Prize

I n 1996, President Bill Clinton appointed me to the board of the John F. Kennedy Center for the Performing Arts. And soon, as part of that job, I would get the chance to co-create and produce an annual event honoring the greatest talents in American comedy.

The Mark Twain Prize has become known as the foremost honor in American humor. Like all great achievements in comedy, there's a huge group of people who want to take credit for it. Finally—right here, right now—I'm going to set the record straight. Get ready for an objective account from me, the author of *The Man Who Made Mark Twain Famous*.

The Kennedy Center had been on my radar for a while because my mother-in-law, Annette Strauss, had been appointed to its board of trustees by President Jimmy Carter in 1981.

One of the signature events it hosts is the Kennedy Center Honors, during which the nation's foremost artists—from singers and instrumentalists to writers and producers to dancers and choreographers to actors and storytellers—are extolled for their achievements. It's one of the most prestigious evenings you can imagine, with tickets that cost up to thousands of dollars, and, usually, the show involves the attendance of a sitting president. That said, some presidents miss the ceremony because of national emergencies. President Carter did not attend in 1979 in the midst of the Iran hostage crisis. President Trump did not attend at any point in the midst of the President Trump crisis.

The night before the Honors, an annual dinner is hosted by the secretary of state for the honorees, their friends and family, and other big names of entertainment and politics. In some ways, the dinner is an even more exclusive and intimate event than the Honors ceremony.

One year, Annette invited me to join her at the dinner—Ronald Reagan was the president, and George Shultz was the secretary of state, so Annette and I were relegated to the "Democrat table." Of course, that was the best place to be: our table had Paul Warfield, Ray Charles, and Stevie Wonder, among others.

My dinner partner was Leontyne Price, the first African American prima donna at the Metropolitan Opera and the first Black American singer to perform opera on television. I confessed what a huge fan of hers I was, despite not being a fan of opera per se. I was especially inspired by her personal story: an underprivileged Black woman from Mississippi who broke barriers to become one of the most recognized singers in the world. I told her as much, and she laughed, demurred, and asked me if I would give opera another chance after I had trouble sitting through *La bohème*. I haven't given it another chance yet. *C'est la vie.*

The honorees that year included Elia Kazan, Katherine Dunham, Virgil Thomson, and Frank Sinatra—but the honoree I was most excited to see was Jimmy Stewart.

Jimmy Stewart was a legend—hell, he was one of my signature impressions in college—so I couldn't resist bringing him my place card to sign. I had him address his signature to my daughters; I only wish I had said one of them was named Cappy.

✦ ✦ ✦

Around that same time, William Jefferson Clinton had taken office as the governor of Arkansas. When he ran for president in 1992, I raised money for him, and at one point got to meet with him and give him my two cents about what was important to the donors and voters in Texas.

At the time, I told him to focus on NAFTA. Months and months later, after becoming president, he tracked me down at a Houston gathering and asked me how he should pitch NAFTA to the unions. This is all to say that the man has a photographic memory. Toward the end of his first term, I got in Senate Minority Leader Daschle's ear and let him know that I was interested in an appointment at the Kennedy Center. The president said, "Hillary's got to approve it." The appointment doesn't require Senate confirmation, which you would think would make the vetting process easier, but Hillary was probably a more meticulous deliberative body than the Senate ever has been.

Soon enough, though, I got the call from Tom: "Congratulations, Cappy. You're going to be appointed to the Kennedy Center." She said yes! Hillary, that is.

In 1997, Murray Horwitz, a playwright, arts administrator, and longtime Vice President of Cultural Programming at NPR, came up with the idea of hosting a big comedy show at the White House. The show would pay tribute to comedy in the same way that the Kennedy Center Honors pays tribute to the arts as a whole. Instead of several honorees, the ceremony would be dedicated to one outstanding comedian at a time. The point of it would be to work to overcome a glaring oversight in American culture—at that point, there was no established awards ceremony dedicated to comedy that could stand alongside what the Oscars mean for movies, what the Grammys mean for music, or what the Tonys mean for theater. The closest equivalent was the American Comedy Awards, a short-lived endeavor that ran from 1987 to 2001 (plus a one-off 2014 revival) and which never achieved the industry status of those other events.

Murray brought the idea to John Schreiber and Mark Krantz, who were partners in the John Schreiber Group, a New York–based entertainment firm that produced live events of all kinds, from concert series to comedy events and Broadway shows.

Together, Murray, John, and Mark went to the White House and pitched the idea to Ann Stock, who was the White House social secretary at the time. Unfortunately, the idea coincided with the early reporting of what would become the all-consuming Monica Lewinsky scandal, so the White House was being extra cautious when it came to public events, and there was no way they were about to green-light a comedy show.

Ann Stock said, "We're not being very funny around here,[6] but soon I'll be moving over to the Kennedy Center, and if you'll take this idea to them, I'll make the introductions."

Soon, John and Mark called Bob and Peter Kaminsky, experienced figures in the entertainment industry. Bob had produced a bunch of prime-time specials for TV, and Peter had been managing editor of the *National Lampoon* and had written for all kinds of comedians. They signed on as part of a deal with Comedy Central, which was going to pony up a million dollars to coproduce and broadcast the show.

Larry Wilker was the president of the Kennedy Center at that point, having been appointed in 1991 after many years of work (and a PhD!) in theater administration. He called me asking if I could join their initial meeting in DC.

I was all for it.

I can think of nothing more American than what comedians do for a living: they utilize freedom of speech to speak truth to power, they make millions laugh, and they bring people of all stripes together. So, we got together for a meeting: me, Larry, Murray, John, Mark, and Peter—Bob was brought in right after.

When it came to justifying why we named the prize after Mark Twain, Larry put it best in a statement to the *Washington Post:* "We

---

6   Also the slogan of *Mad TV*.

tried to think of someone who had a particular nexus with American humor. Twain is one of the greatest humorists and social commentators, and a name that would be recognized."

We had our show concept, we had the Kennedy Center as our venue, and we had our title. Then came the pivotal decision: Who would be the first recipient of the Mark Twain Prize? We knew that if we made an ill-advised decision, it could end up being the *only* Mark Twain Prize. If this was going to become an annual event, the inaugural show would have to go spectacularly, and that would depend heavily on the honoree we selected.

We needed someone with a big enough name to be a draw in and of themselves, both to sell tickets to the live event and to attract viewers on television. We needed someone who was respected enough in the entertainment world to get a bunch of high-profile presenters to show up and honor their career. And we needed someone with enough gravitas to live up to the intended purpose of the award: that is, an out-and-out living comedy legend.

With all of that in mind, we decided to honor Richard Pryor. He broke barriers as a Black comedian, as a provocateur, and as someone who was willing to get deeply personal on stage. The likes of Jerry Seinfeld, Chris Rock, and Dave Chappelle consistently cited him as a major influence. And he has since been ranked #1 in lists of the greatest stand-up comedians of all time by both Comedy Central and *Rolling Stone*.

John Schreiber also gave a great explanation: "When you think about the continuum of comedy over the last two hundred years, Twain is seminal, then Lenny Bruce, and for our generation…Pryor is it. He exposed race, the confrontation between the sexes, in a way everyone could understand the comedy and tragedy of our lives."

Richard Pryor said it all in a statement after the announcement: "I feel great about accepting this prize. It is nice to be regarded on par with a great white man. Now that's funny! Seriously though, two things people throughout history have had in common are hatred and humor. I am proud that like Mark Twain, I have been able to use humor to lessen people's hatred."

✦ ✦ ✦

In September of 1998, we announced our selection and scheduled the ceremony for October (then to be aired on Comedy Central the following January).

It was a star-studded lineup from our very first endeavor—Whoopi Goldberg, Damon Wayans, Morgan Freeman, Robin Williams, and Chris Rock, among many others, performing routines and paying tribute to Richard Pryor. Mark Krantz promised that despite Pryor's raunchy history, it would be a respectful night: "The guidelines we have given them is that the performances should be personal, directed to Richard…. It will be a tasteful evening, a fairly clean evening."

And if you're wondering how that went, remember what happened the last time I placed content limitations on defiant comedians. To be fair, you couldn't have a proper tribute to Richard Pryor if everyone were on their best behavior—but Chris Rock in particular broke new ground on the Kennedy Center stage with his liberal use of the f-word *and* the n-word. You can sum up the provocativeness of Rock's routine with this joke, in which he imagined what Richard Pryor would say if he met Mark Twain:

"(He'd) probably say, 'I really enjoy your work.' And what would Mark Twain say to Richard Pryor? He'd probably say, 'N*****, pick up my bag.'"

That joke made some of the stuffier people in the room uncomfortable, which is pretty much the biggest compliment you could give Chris. Thankfully, the event was *not* broadcast live, as it never has been, so we never had to figure out who would foot the bill in the event of a standards violation. You can't get away with much when the FCC is literally two miles away.

The show went well in terms of its content, but as a fundraising event for the Kennedy Center, it had been a rocky start. I had to buy out literally a third of the concert hall to make sure the seats were filled. I got nervous about how the powers-that-be would receive the night with just about every joke. The funnier the joke, the more concerned I became about getting in trouble. As usual.

But it was still a lot of fun, with so many beautiful moments as everyone gave Richard Pryor his due. Janie and I also hosted a nice little dinner before the show with about twenty people in the African Room at the Kennedy Center. We still had a bunch of kinks to work out, but I thought at the very least we had a durable proof-of-concept to continue the tradition.

The next morning, we had an executive committee meeting at the Kennedy Center. All in all, we had lost a little over $100,000 on the whole endeavor, but that was not unexpected for an undertaking of that scale the first time around. To me, it had clear potential, and I was willing to fight for it, as I had already made clear with all those tickets I bought. Jim Johnson was the chairman of the board, and he asked me to give a report on how it went. I emphasized all the highlights of the evening and thoroughly glossed over the controversy.

Some of the folks on the board had been enthusiastic about the idea from the very beginning. Others, like Buffy Cafritz and Alma Powell (spouses of Bill Cafritz and Colin Powell, respectively), didn't think another annual to-do was necessary because they had just started the Kennedy Center's Spring Gala, another celebrity-heavy large-scale event. Most everyone seemed to be in agreement: our first attempt hadn't been perfect, but we could see how the Mark Twain Prize could grow into something bigger and better with time and effort. But there was one person on the board who didn't say a word: Jean Kennedy Smith, the ambassador to Ireland and, more importantly, John F. Kennedy's sister.

I did my best to make the case in favor of pressing on, and then we held a vote. To my delight, I had convinced most of the skeptics: Buffy and Alma both voted in favor of bringing the Mark Twain Prize back. In fact, it was almost unanimous: only Jean Kennedy Smith voted against it.

After the executive committee meeting was over, Jim Johnson approached me grimly. "You know, I'm so sorry, Cappy," he said. "Jean Kennedy Smith is the president's sister—if she's against it, it's not going to happen."

I knew he was right. There was only one course of action left: I made a beeline to Jean, and I made my plea: "Ambassador, a lot of people have worked really hard to make the Mark Twain Prize happen, and we would really like to see it through into the coming years."

She had a fair response: "Well, my brother would have been horrified to hear the n-word and the f-word said on the stage bearing his name."

I couldn't argue with that, or at least, I wasn't going to out loud. "Ambassador, you're absolutely right," I said. "I thought that was very inappropriate." Which wasn't a lie. I just conveniently left out that I also thought it was very funny.

I also tried to frame the evening positively: "Respectfully, I also think your brother would have loved to hear the booming laughter on the stage bearing his name, not to mention all the young people who came out to the Kennedy Center for the first time for the show."

In an effort to convince her it was an honor worth continuing, I started listing every palatable, inoffensive, older comedian I could come up with: Dick Van Dyke! Jonathan Winters! Carl Reiner! I proposed that we could use the prestige of the Kennedy Center to lift up the funny people who brought Americans joy for a lifetime.

Finally, Jean said: "Well, let me think about it."

I pushed just a little bit more. "If you think we should keep awarding the prize, please change your vote. Because if you don't change your vote, it's just not going to happen."

She went up to Jim Johnson, whispered in his ear, and changed her vote.

At the board meeting that followed, Jim announced that the executive committee of the Kennedy Center had voted unanimously to bring the Mark Twain Prize back for another year. I was elated. We would get the chance to showcase the career of another comedy luminary, and it was not lost on me that this was happening—and I was getting to stay involved—in spite of the fact that I had let Chris Rock storm the Kennedy Center stage uncensored. (In the years since, the Kennedy Center has made it a policy not to censor comedians when they take the stage.) It was a victory on so many levels.

And that dinner for twenty people that Janie and I hosted? It would go on to become a tradition of the Kennedy Center in and of itself. The guest list has grown each year, and when it reached around a hundred attendees, the Kennedy Center's VP of Development, Marie Mattson, came to me and suggested I help turn it into a fundraiser, which I had always wanted it to be in any case. Along with AOL founder and Kennedy Center board member Jim Kimsey, we were the first chairs of the rehearsal dinner as a fundraiser hosted by the Kennedy Center. They also kept me on as an emcee for the evening every year, which was a very different kind of hosting.

Now the Kennedy Center hosts the dinner for something like fifteen hundred people every year, right before the show—and it's become one of their biggest fundraisers.

I was elated that both the rehearsal dinner and the Mark Twain Prize were taking the next step from a one-off experiment to an annual tradition. I felt it could be so valuable to take a moment—even once a year—in the middle of the nation's capital, to drop politics, put our differences aside, and spend an evening honoring someone who makes us laugh in spite of it all.

The goal of the Mark Twain Prize, as I saw it, was to remind us who we are and what we have to celebrate in the uproarious world of American comedy.

CHAPTER FIFTEEN

Winters Is Coming/Carl's Hour

With the Mark Twain Prize successfully, if precariously, renewed by the Kennedy Center, we were tasked with selecting honorees for the next couple of years who could reasonably follow Richard Pryor. We would need to choose people who had achieved a level of impact on the world of comedy that was at least comparable to that of Richard Pryor, while at the same time being "safe" enough to assuage anyone at the Kennedy Center who might have been made anxious by the vulgarity of the initial ceremony.

We landed on two legends: in 1999, we honored Jonathan Winters, and in 2000, we honored Carl Reiner (it was a coincidence that they were among the names I'd used to change Jean Kennedy Smith's mind).

By the time we announced that Jonathan Winters would be the second recipient of the Mark Twain Prize, he was seventy-three years old and had enjoyed a career in comedy spanning five decades. Over the years, he had appeared on countless television shows and in numerous movies, had recorded over twenty comedy albums, and in the later days of his career, had lent his shape-shifting voice to all kinds of animated characters.

His handle on improvisational comedy was nothing short of masterful—it was no surprise that he and Robin Williams were close. I grew up watching Winters on TV and listening to his records, so it was a dream come true to get to meet him and watch him rehearse for the show.

The rehearsals typically take place the day before the event itself or the morning of, and the presenters just want to get a feel for the stage, judge the distance of the teleprompter, and see where the honoree will be sitting (in a box up and to the left from the stage). Usually there are a handful of people in the audience: writers for the show, maintenance staff setting up, and people involved in the production who are working to optimize the tech setup. Over the years, I've seen some of the funniest people in America approach rehearsals in dramatically different ways. Some of them want their routines and speeches to scroll through the teleprompter as they read them (without necessarily performing them) out loud. Some want to study their remarks silently, so that nobody in the audience hears a joke before its debut at the show.

More often than not for the honoree, this would be a quiet moment in the rehearsal, where the performer stares into space and waits to be told to move again. But Jonathan Winters was standing on a stage, and he technically had an audience, so he did his thing, breaking out his classic bits for the handful of people in the room. I distinctly remember him reenacting his baseball act, a slapstick routine where he pantomimes the moves and mimics the sounds of a pitcher. His performance, even in a rehearsal and to a small crowd, was full tilt.

(A decade later, I saw Steve Martin do something similar. Tina Fey was being honored with the prize, and Martin was doing his walk-through. But instead of just scrolling through what he wanted to say, he started delivering it, refining it, and he didn't stop until the seven or eight people, who were really in the theater to do other jobs, were rolling with laughter.)

In fact, if anything, Jonathan Winters's rehearsal was a funnier performance than the one he gave at the actual ceremony; he was a little more emotional and reflective when he was actually receiving the honor (he welled up a lot). He still told some jokes, though:

"I played some pretty good-sized pads in my career. I don't think I've ever played a thing this size. And this high, the chandeliers…my wife said, 'Could we get *one*?' I said, 'I wouldn't want to press that on the people; they're there for a reason, and we live in a trailer!'"

And he claimed he'd met up with an old buddy from Ohio named Wally, and after a long, rambling conversation, Wally had said, "I haven't seen you since '43. What do you do now?" Winters said, "Why, I'm in television." Wally paused for a moment and said, "You know, Mary Beth's got a Zenith, I wonder if you could take a look at it."

And then he closed with some genuine gratitude for the folks in the room, and one last joke: "I want to thank all the people that suited up and came…it's been a fabulous night, truly, for all of us, and I hope for all of you. I hope to come back. I always enjoy seeing the Washington Memorial, to know that it'll finally be finished…I wonder what Washington would think."

He then pantomimed Washington looking up in astonishment and throwing a spear: "'Good God, Martha, look! Pick it up and throw it!'"

After the evening's festivities came to a close, Winters went out into the lobby of the Four Seasons Hotel and took people's suggestions for ad-libbed routines. No matter what word or phrase they threw at him, he couldn't be stumped. Most importantly, it didn't matter whether he was in front of a television audience of millions or an empty room with a couple of stagehands—he was a kindhearted, eager-to-please entertainer.

✦ ✦ ✦

And so to 2000, when Carl Reiner was the third recipient of the Mark Twain Prize.

Reiner had been a formative figure in the earliest days of television comedy, co-writing and starring in *Your Show of Shows* and *Caesar's Hour* with Sid Caesar, as well as creating and acting in *The Dick Van Dyke Show*. He was also key in launching the film career of Steve Martin, directing his vehicles *The Jerk*, *Dead Men Don't Wear Plaid*, *The Man with Two Brains*, and *All of Me*.

For the ceremony, we were able to gather some of the most legendary people with whom Carl Reiner had worked to pay him tribute, including Martin, Van Dyke, and Mary Tyler Moore. We also included younger comedians who had been influenced by Reiner, including Jerry Seinfeld, just a couple of years removed from the finale of his iconic sitcom.

Seinfeld said, "I think that Carl Reiner is funnier than Mark Twain," and Carl had already proved that point early on in the evening: there had been a malfunction with the sound system, and while the folks behind the scenes scrambled to fix it, he bellowed from the balcony, "Does anyone have four double-A batteries?" Even though he was last on the lineup, Carl Reiner found a way to get the first laugh of the night.

When he took the stage, he was still funny, but he couldn't mask the depths of his emotion as he thanked his family and friends.

"Something like this is thrown at you, your hands sweat, your chest throbs, and you're very nervous. And I am that. But I'm also very thankful that I've lived the kind of a life that allows me to have a family like that and an evening like this!"

From there, Carl acknowledged that he "stood on the shoulders of some giants" to make it all the way to the Mark Twain Prize: "Sid Caesar…I stood on his shoulders. Steve Martin, I stood on his broad shoulders. Dick Van Dyke, his broad shoulders. Mary Tyler Moore… her great legs, not the broad shoulders."

After thanking just about every major player involved in the ceremony and his career, Carl Reiner started to exit the stage to his playoff music, but before he could get halfway to the wings, he remembered one last thing he wanted to say, waving off the instrumental and gesturing toward the Twain Prize bust.

(A note on the physical prize itself: it's a copy of an 1884 bronze bust of Mark Twain's head [and by extension, his poofy hair and iconic mustache]. The bust was originally sculpted by the artist Karl Gerhardt, who relied upon Samuel Clemens for a bunch of jobs and commissions. It stands a little over a foot tall, and it's heavy, which I know better than anybody because I'm often the guy responsible for lugging it around.)

"The stage manager before said that I shouldn't try to pick this up; it's very heavy, we'll send it to you…. In Spain, in the Coruña Film Festival, *Dead Men Don't Wear Plaid* won the award as the best comedy, I as the best director. And they said, 'We'll send you the award! It's a very large award!' Did they send it? Did I get it? Never." And with that, Carl Reiner snatched the Mark Twain Prize right off the stage.

✦ ✦ ✦

That year marked a major milestone: in what would become an annual tradition (one that I would come to organize with the White House social secretary), and thanks to the willingness of Bill Clinton, Carl was the first winner of the Mark Twain Prize to be invited to visit the president of the United States in the Oval Office.

Shortly before the visit, Carl called me and said that he wanted to bring his brother Charlie to the meeting. Charlie was in his early eighties, had been diagnosed with cancer, and was a veteran of World War II. And not just any veteran—he was a combat veteran who fought in eleven major battles. In addition to that service to his country, Charlie was also the guy who pointed his brother in the direction of a free acting workshop that changed the course of Carl's career, so he was also partially responsible for sparking Carl Reiner's career.

I was tasked with bringing Carl's group—Charlie; his son Rob Reiner; Dick Van Dyke; Mary Tyler Moore; Jerry Seinfeld, and Jerry's wife, Jessica—into the Oval Office individually and introducing them to the president. Charlie, who was in a wheelchair, was first to come in, with Carl pushing him. I entered with them, and started to speak: "Mister President, this is—"

"Oh, Cappy, I know who this is," the president said.

And with that, President Clinton got down on his knee, took both of Charlie's hands, looked him directly in the eyes, and said,

"Charlie, I'm so honored to meet you and to have you in the Oval Office. As you might imagine, I get a lot of guests here, but there's no more honored guest than you. I'm so thankful for your service; I understand you were part of one of the first waves of soldiers dispatched on the beach at Normandy. You truly have given me an honor by coming here today."

He continued to praise Charlie in such beautifully effusive language, in a way that only Bill Clinton could—I could feel the genuine sense of pride and patriotism that Charlie inspired in the president. And I knew Carl Reiner could feel it too, because we were both choking up. It was one of those rare, beautiful instances where you understand that you're experiencing a once-in-a-lifetime moment.

CHAPTER SIXTEEN

We Can Still Be Funny

On May 1, 2001, the Kennedy Center announced that we would be honoring Whoopi Goldberg as the fourth recipient of the Mark Twain Prize that October. She was the first woman and second person of color to receive the prize. She'd had a remarkable career: after coming up in the world of theater and improv, she put herself on the map with her one-woman show on Broadway in the mid-1980s, which led to her getting cast as the lead in Steven Spielberg's film adaptation of *The Color Purple*. After that, she never stopped doing groundbreaking work, from theater to film to television to comedy. She's always getting out of her comfort zone—whether it's in her art or in debating conservatives on *The View*.

More than simply being entertaining, her work was a force for good in the world: it was an inspiration to generations of Black female comedians, actors, and artists of all stripes, and, together with Bill Crystal and Robin Williams, she had done phenomenal work with the charity Comic Relief USA. She was, and is, an accomplished woman of many talents who embodies the tremendous value that comedians bring to American culture, which is why we were delighted to select her and anticipated an amazing evening in October.

Then, just a month before the ceremony, everything changed. The Kennedy Center sits just a couple of miles from the Pentagon, and with the 9/11 attacks so fresh in our hearts and minds, we had to ask ourselves if there was an acceptable way to go about our business of funny or would this event be too much too soon?

In the days following the attacks, late-night comedy institutions like *The Late Show with David Letterman*, *The Daily Show with Jon Stewart*, and *Late Night with Conan O'Brien* slowly came back, but with somber monologues and serious interviews about the news. The Emmys ended up getting pushed back twice: once the weekend after the attacks and once in early October after the launch of the War on Afghanistan. And in a September 14 article from the *Baltimore Sun* titled "When Will It Feel Right to Feel Right Again?" an editor for the satire publication *The Onion* was simply quoted as saying: "None of us are feeling funny."

When *Saturday Night Live* returned to air at the end of September, the show's cold open perfectly illustrated the uncertainty among comedians about how to proceed. Mayor Rudy Giuliani appeared with members of New York's Police Department and Fire Department and paid tribute to the heroes who were on the ground that day. Then, after a somber performance of "The Boxer" by Paul Simon, *SNL* executive producer Lorne Michaels went on stage and thanked everyone for being there. Giuliani, in turn, emphasized the value of the show reestablishing some sense of normalcy: "*Saturday Night Live* is one of our great New York City institutions, and that's why it's important for you to do your show tonight."

Lorne said, "Can we be funny?" to which Giuliani said, "Why start now?"

This seemed to light a way for us, and we decided that the show must go on. We had seriously considered cancelling the ceremony, but the Mark Twain Prize is all about celebrating the practitioners of laughter and the healing power they bring. It seemed more important than ever.

Still, even as Whoopi agreed to remain on the show, she struggled with how to approach her remarks. As a lifelong New Yorker, she felt extra pressure to get it right—she'd be funny, of course, but *how* funny? First, though, we had to get her there. Even before 9/11, Whoopi had harbored a fear of flying. When she came to Washington for the rehearsal and performance, she commuted the way she always does: on her tour bus.

On top of everything else, there was a political challenge: Whoopi was an outspoken critic of President George W. Bush, and she had no interest in meeting him. Ultimately, she was one of the few honorees whom I didn't take to the Oval Office. Her lack of interest didn't make any big waves, though; in the midst of the recovery, people had more pressing things on their minds.

The ceremony took place on October 15, 2001. Just over a month had passed since the attacks, and just over a week had passed since the United States had invaded Afghanistan. It was a really scary, chaotic moment in history, and it felt like another disaster could strike at any moment. And sure enough, it did.

Literally *that day*, Tom Daschle informed the press that anthrax had been found in packages mailed to his office. Tom was supposed to attend the ceremony that night, as he did every year, but with all the panic and media attention and security protocols he was enduring, the optics of the Senate majority leader laughing it up at a comedy show would not be ideal, and he gave me a call to let me know as much. But to give you an idea of how *nice* Tom Daschle is, he offered in lieu of his attendance to meet with Whoopi, and he and his wife, Linda, even came to the pre-show dinner that Janie and I hosted. Would *you* do that the day you got anthrax in the mail?

✦ ✦ ✦

With the country in crisis, it's difficult to imagine worse circumstances for comedy, especially in front of an audience who had spent the last month in close proximity to an American crisis. It would take nothing short of a pitch-perfect, riotous performance to get laughs in that room.

In other words, we needed Robin Williams and Billy Crystal. Luckily, we had them.

To kick off the show, Billy and Robin burst onto the stage, with Robin donning a gas mask and a kilt. The gas mask was an overt reference to the post-9/11 panic; the kilt, who knows—because it was Robin Williams? In a moment when everyone felt unsure whether it was okay to laugh, he burst onto the stage with an unabashedly hilarious performance that gave the audience the permission they needed. In the face of a hand-wringing audience and public, Robin flipped his kilt up and joked that he "wanted to give the first row a thrill." Billy, playing the straight man, looked into the crowd and deadpanned, "We're glad to be here to...look for anyone suspicious." Then Robin wandered around the stage in a kilt and mask, searching for whoever that could be.

I should note Robin delivered half of his lines in an inexplicable, stereotypical Scottish accent. Even the lines that weren't (completely) facetious: "I'm dressed like this because Whoopi, you'd understand. You've done outrageous things in your life. You are up there with your giant posse!"

Billy said, "What was the last word?"

"Don't even start on that one! We've lost many a good man! Don't go there unless you're prepared to stay for a while!"

By this point, Robin's accent was starting to slip, and Billy asked: "What are you, a pirate?"

And Robin replied, "Arrr, it's changin' as we speak."

At one point, Robin crouched down behind Billy and recited a bunch of one-liners in different accents that Billy deftly lip-synced while gesticulating wildly to demonstrate how beloved Whoopi was around the world. The crowd loved it. This was an achievement, given the circumstances.

The rest of the evening's entertainers didn't disappoint, either. The show was hosted by the great Harry Belafonte and featured performances by a diverse array of comedians: Tommy Davidson, Cedric the Entertainer, Alan King, Caroline Rhea, Wanda Sykes, Bruce Vilanch, and Chris Tucker. In other words: Whoopi's friends, her collaborators, and Chris Tucker. (*Rush Hour 2* was huge that year.)

By the time Whoopi took the stage to accept the honor, the audience had already made it clear: they were ready to laugh again, even and especially at jokes that acknowledged the dark feelings that were pervading the country. And Whoopi gave a fantastic speech. She was funny, of course, but she also opened up to the audience—and, upon the show's broadcast, the nation—about the feelings she wrestled with as she debated whether to attend the show:

"I held myself under a microscope. It wasn't that I didn't like what I saw. It was just that I wasn't sure…I realized that on behalf of all those folks I spent time with in New York, these things are important. We must pick ourselves up by our bootstrings and laugh. We have to."

It was a vulnerable moment, and deeply relatable to anyone who wasn't sure how to move on. Then she emphasized the public service role she felt that she held as a comedian—to make people laugh even during the most daunting of hardships—which is why, ultimately, it was okay to have the ceremony: "I'm not embarrassed now. I feel like a firefighter or a policeman. As an American, that's what I have to offer: dirty jokes and bad language."

It's true: everyone has a role to play. And while we couldn't hold a candle to the real heroes—the survivors, the first responders, the newly enlisted military personnel, and everyone else who played a direct part in the recovery—we *could* give those people a couple hours of entertainment, make them laugh, and hopefully help them forget the troubles of life for just a moment.

The Mark Twain Prize always exemplifies that mission, and that was never clearer to me than in 2001.

CHAPTER SEVENTEEN

Broadcasting Legends of Broadcasting

As the years passed and the Mark Twain Prize became more established as an American tradition, we had the privilege of honoring three more comedy stars, each of whom had a wildly different impact on the world of entertainment: Bob Newhart, Lily Tomlin, and Lorne Michaels.

We paid tribute to Bob Newhart in 2002. Bob had achieved tremendous success in just about all of comedy's forms. When his first album, *The Button-Down Mind of Bob Newhart*, was released in 1960, it was the first comedy album ever to reach number one on the Billboard charts—and for fourteen weeks! He had appeared regularly on television, starring in four TV shows with his name on them: *The Bob Newhart Show* (a variety show, 1961–1962), another *The Bob Newhart Show* (a sitcom, 1972–1978), *Newhart* (perhaps his most famous sitcom, 1982–1990), and *Bob* (a sitcom, 1992–1993). (No disrespect to Bob Newhart, but his prodigious creativity didn't extend to his naming of television shows.)

Beyond that, he had appeared in a bunch of movies, toured all over the country, and popularized iconic comedy routines like the "one-sided telephone call," which has become a trope in movies and television: the audience hears only one end of a conversation out-of-context, and the laughs come from filling in the blanks.

At the ceremony, we got the chance to showcase comedy legends from every era of Bob's nearly half-century career. From Richard Belzer to Jane Curtin to Kelsey Grammer to Bernie Mac to Julia Sweeney to the Smothers Brothers—to the late, great Don Rickles and Tim Conway—the sheer variety of entertainers who graced that stage demonstrated just how many lives and careers Bob Newhart had touched over the years.

Incidentally, Bob was the first recipient of the Mark Twain Prize to visit President George W. Bush in the Oval Office. I don't agree with just about any of President Bush's politics. But in meeting Bob, Bush was nothing but cordial and nice. Just like his father was, George W. Bush is a gentleman in person. Bush showed us around the Oval Office, pointed out the paintings, as well as a great bust of Winston Churchill by Jacob Epstein. Tim Conway joined us on that tour and had all of us in stitches the entire time.

Speaking of Tim Conway leaving us in stitches, a big highlight from that year came at the rehearsal dinner, which took place at the Four Seasons Hotel in a private dining room. A bunch of Bob Newhart's famous buddies gave toasts in his honor, and Tim Conway was last in line. When his turn came, he got up, raised his glass, took a good look around the room, and finally said: "I've never had salmon run through me quite this fast." Then he sprinted out of the room and got the biggest laugh of that night, which was no small task.

✦ ✦ ✦

The next year, in 2003, Lily Tomlin was our honoree. She too had achieved astounding success in comedy, television, and film over the course of several decades. She had risen to prominence as a cast member on *Rowan & Martin's Laugh-In*, starred in half a dozen comedy specials, led multiple Broadway shows, appeared in a plethora of feature films, and received plenty of accolades in the process, including a Grammy, two Tonys, and six Emmys.

Beyond Lily's status as a brilliantly funny comedic icon, she is also one of the nicest people I've ever had the pleasure to meet. Throughout the years, she and I have become good friends—and I couldn't be luckier. She's as gracious as she is hilarious…and she has a Mark Twain Prize, for God's sake!

The ceremony featured her close friends and contemporaries in Hollywood—like Jane Fonda,[7] Dolly Parton, and Elaine Stritch—along with younger comedians who grew up on her work, like Dave Chappelle and George Lopez. And, in the greatest coup of all, we booked a frequent television co-star of Lily Tomlin, a legend herself, and one of the first women in Hollywood to reject the type of body shaming that had become the norm: The Muppets' Miss Piggy.

One of the most emotional moments of the ceremony was provided by Ellen DeGeneres, who got the chance to thank Lily for the support that she had given to the gay community over her career. Both of them had faced the challenge of living as gay women in comedy and entertainment, though in different generations. Both had received offers from *Time* magazine to come out on its cover early in their careers—Lily had turned it down in 1975, fearing a backlash and the reaction of her mother; Ellen decided to do it in 1997 and *did* get significant backlash, but she paved the way for other public figures to come out in a safer and more understanding environment.

Lily would go on to pay tribute to Ellen when we gave her the Mark Twain Prize nearly ten years later. She compared Ellen to Mark Twain's signature character, Huckleberry Finn—praising her as a "folk hero," and acknowledging the bravery it took for her to come out publicly: "Like Huck, who had the courage to confront the code of convention, rather than betray a friend, you, Ellen, had the same

---

7   Incidentally, Jane Fonda was my dinner partner at the rehearsal dinner. I think
     she had more martinis than bites of food that night…but she was as elegant
     and beautiful as she was buzzed.

courage to confront convention and not betray yourself or your sense of destiny. And the world would never be the same."

In addition to giving comedy stars their due, another beautiful thing the Mark Twain Prize does is give collaborators, friends, and mentors the chance to express gratitude for one another on the public stage, and when it comes full circle like it did for Lily and Ellen, it's a joy to witness.

Cast photo from the Mark Twain Prize ceremony for Lily Tomlin.
Lily pictured at center, sitting on Cappy's knee.

✦　✦　✦

In 2004, the honor went to Lorne Michaels—an honoree whose work I had gotten to see up close and personal in the early days of *Saturday Night Live*.

Nearly three decades earlier, in 1977, I attended a reception in New York for UT football star Earl Campbell. There, I ran into my friend Coach Darrell Royal, whom I had bonded with at several Willie Nelson concerts. He told me he had tickets to see *Saturday Night Live* that night with Willie as the musical guest, and I told him I'd give my left you-know-what to join him. He told me I could come along with no strings attached.

So, with a skip in my step and my left you-know-what intact, I joined Darrell, his wife, Edith, and their friends, Jack and Joanne Crosby, at 30 Rock, where we watched Willie Nelson smoking dope on stage during the dress rehearsal, and then came the show itself, hosted by Mary Kay Place.

The energy was *electric*. And NBC wasn't even owned by GE back then! On the same stage as a ragtag group of comedy legends-in-waiting, you've got Willie Nelson singing "Blue Eyes Crying in the Rain." My eyes may not be blue, and they may not have been crying, but damn if they weren't popping out of my head that whole hour and a half.

Before our high from watching the show could wear off, Coach had already told us we were invited to the after-party. If you know *anything* about *SNL* lore, you know the only experience more off-the-rails than seeing the show in its prime with the original cast is going to the after-party with the original cast.

Appropriately enough, the party was at the Lone Star Cafe, a ridiculously heightened honkytonk away from home on the corner of Fifth Avenue and Thirteenth Street. This place had not one, not two, but *three* Texas flags emblazoned on its facade. Shoot, even the Texas Capitol only has one!

Willie played for about an hour, and then, toward the end of his set, he introduced that evening's headliner. He said, "There's this new group I wanna bring up onto the stage to play for you all. Please welcome...the Blues Brothers."

Here's the thing. The Blues Brothers hadn't even made their TV debut yet. At that point, they were just *Some* Blues Brothers. But when John Belushi and Dan Aykroyd stumbled onto the stage that night wearing their soon-to-be signature black ties and sunglasses, I had no idea that I was witnessing the genesis of a legendary comedy and music duo.

But I did know I was seeing something special. They sang "Soul Man" months before they'd sing it on national television. The crowd went crazy and started chanting for more. Belushi defiantly responded: "F**k you! We only know one song!" Taking the note, the crowd instead chanted for an encore of "Soul Man." And we got it.

Things went on like that until about three or four in the morning. It was one of the wildest days/nights/early mornings of my life. I saw the Blues Brothers before the Blues Brothers were the Blues Brothers.

✦ ✦ ✦

We were no less excited to honor Lorne with the Mark Twain Prize in 2004. Lorne's award had an interesting distinction. As of 2021, he is the only recipient of the Mark Twain Prize for American Humor who was born and raised outside the United States. We justified this for a few reasons. First of all, he was born in Canada, which is basically a giant suburb of the United States. Second, he became an American citizen in 1987, and we weren't talking about the American presidency here; we felt you didn't need to be a natural-born citizen to be an American humorist. Third, and most importantly, even if you dispute the first two points, the Mark Twain Prize honors American *humor,* not necessarily American humor*ists,* and Lorne's impact on this country's comedic history as the executive producer of *Saturday Night Live* is second to none.

Given *SNL*'s central position in American comedy, we had a pretty incredible lineup to pay tribute to Lorne and the staggering thirty-year run of the show. Cast members like Dan Aykroyd, Darrell Hammond, and Tina Fey were hysterical. All-time great guests like Steve Martin, Paul Simon, and Christopher Walken were inspiring.

And we even had politicians from across the political spectrum, like Senators John McCain (R-AZ) and Chris Dodd (D-CT), who joked that *SNL* helped politicians temper their egos because "politics is show business for ugly people."

Steve Martin quipped about Lorne, "Knowing that you've guided one of the most important comedy shows ever to be on television, knowing that you've fathered three beautiful children, knowing that you deserve this award tonight, I feel nothing but pride—not respect, not admiration, just pride."

Dan Aykroyd rightly called him "the primary satirical voice of the country." And Tina Fey remarked that *SNL* had been "the pinnacle of sketch comedy for thirty years." It goes to show just how universal the appeal of *SNL* has always been—and no one person deserves more credit for that than Lorne.

Then came Lorne's speech. To be honest, we weren't sure what we were going to get. After all, we're normally paying tribute to actors and stand-ups—Lorne wasn't really a performer. Would the speech be awkward?

We needn't have worried—Lorne gave a great speech, acknowledging how much of his success he owed to the people who worked on his show, but with wit:

"We did a show last Saturday night in New York," he said, "and we'll do a show this Saturday night as well. And last weekend, in the final production meeting just before we went on the air, I looked around the room and saw all the writers, and the cast, the director, the designers, the musicians, my fellow producers, and all of the production staff. And I thought: they have all worked so hard and so long this week, and are about to go out there and give everything they have for this week's show. And yet, I'm the one getting on the plane tomorrow with my tuxedo and heading to Washington to be honored. And I thought…yes, that's the way it should be."

And then he doubled down on the gratitude and the bit: "I can't possibly thank everyone who performed here tonight, but they are my friends. And I know nothing will mean as much to them as thanking them individually with a personal phone call…in the next week or two…or at least, having an assistant leave word."

Then, in a moment for the ages, the *SNL* "Goodbyes" theme began to play behind Lorne, and he explained why: "I'm not very good at ending things. It turns out that the only thing that has remained the same over the years at *SNL* is the 'Goodnights.' The host thanking the musical guest, the cast milling around the stage, while credits roll, and I can't think of any better way to end this show than to have all of the cast of *SNL* who are here tonight join the performers on stage."

They did, in what felt like one of the most star-studded family reunions you could put together. Which I guess is another way of describing the Mark Twain Prize.

CHAPTER EIGHTEEN

Hopes Dashed

A few great years for the Twain Prize were punctuated by one of the worst nights of my life: election night, 2004.

I was still Senate Minority Leader Tom Daschle's national finance chair and the chairman of DASHPAC, but he was facing a tough reelection battle against former US Representative John Thune. Before he ultimately decided to run for reelection in 2004, Tom had considered a campaign for the Democratic nomination for president. Ultimately, he decided against it, feeling he could do more good in the Senate. It's a shame that he didn't run, because I believe he could have gotten the nomination, defeated Bush, and been an outstanding leader for the country.

Thune, a self-proclaimed Christian conservative, had already won statewide a few times, having represented South Dakota's at-large district. Thune had run for Senate two years earlier, and after a protracted recount, lost by just 532 votes to Senator Tim Johnson, demonstrating South Dakota's continuing rightward shift. Daschle had endured some tight races in South Dakota before too, both when he was a US Representative and in his first Senate election. So, 2004 was shaping up to be an uncomfortably close election, both for Daschle and nationally between Bush and Kerry, and any given fundraiser, rally, or news cycle could potentially make or break the campaign.

Tom's race was a nail-biter. I didn't even have time to be stressed about the presidential election, which was also a nail-biter. The stakes were enormously high for us: depending on the outcome of the night, Tom could end up becoming the Senate majority leader under a Kerry administration or an unemployed private citizen under a second term of Bush.

The night dragged on and on, and past midnight the race was still too close to call. Almost all the counties were tallied—we were still waiting for the results from the Native American reservations to come in, but Thune was ahead by a few thousand votes. Then, around half past one in the morning, Tom's wife, Linda, asked me to come up to the family suite of the hotel.

It was over. In the room, everyone was in tears. The race had been called for Thune, and not by much. (In the end, it was a margin of 4,508 votes.)

It was bad enough that it felt like the good guys lost, but over the years, Tom had become a close friend, and being in the trenches of multiple campaigns with him had made that bond even stronger. I've never believed in the inherent goodness of a politician more than I did with Tom Daschle. (Mothers-in-law notwithstanding, of course.) I was invested in his success—not just as a fundraiser, but as a friend.

✦ ✦ ✦

Though Tom never became the forty-fourth president himself, he did lead me to throw my support behind the guy who did. During the 2008 presidential race, I was an early supporter of Senator Obama's campaign (because Senator Daschle was an early supporter, and if Tom tells me to do something, I do it). I became one of Obama's major fundraisers on the National Finance Committee.

I was co-chairing a fundraiser in Dallas when I got a call from the Obama campaign. The guy said, "Unfortunately, Senator Obama can't attend this fundraiser, but we're sending a surrogate."

All right, sure. Who was the temp?

"We're sending Bill Clinton."

Wow. The senator couldn't make it, but we got the president instead. On the day of the event, I put some Cuban cigars in a baggy with my business card, handed the package to an aide, and I said surreptitiously, "Just tell the president these are contraband."

A couple of weeks later, I got a letter from him: "Dear Cappy: It was great to see you and thanks for the gift. Fidel and I salute you! Best, Bill."

WILLIAM JEFFERSON CLINTON

10/16/09

CHAPTER NINETEEN

A Texan and Two New Yorkers

As we closed out the first decade of the Mark Twain Prize, we got to honor three men who had reached unparalleled heights in their comedic careers: Steve Martin, Neil Simon, and Billy Crystal.

Steve Martin became the eighth person to receive the Mark Twain Prize in 2005. And if there's such a thing as an ideal candidate for the Mark Twain Prize, he was it.

Martin started his career in the late 1960s as a TV writer for *The Smothers Brothers Comedy Hour*, before spending the early 1970s performing stand-up comedy on shows like *The Tonight Show Starring Johnny Carson*, *The Gong Show*, and *Saturday Night Live*, among others. Not long afterward, he started putting out comedy albums like *Let's Get Small* and *A Wild and Crazy Guy*, both of which went platinum in the United States and won the Grammy for Best Comedy Recording. Beginning in 1979 with Carl Reiner's *The Jerk*, Martin became a bona fide movie star, appearing in classics like *Little Shop of Horrors*; *Planes, Trains, and Automobiles*; *Parenthood*; and *Father of the Bride* throughout the 1980s and 1990s. He had hosted the Oscars in 2001 and 2003, and his two most recent films before the Mark Twain Prize were the highest grossing of his career: *Bringing Down the House* and *Cheaper by the Dozen*.

Steve had a full crew of show business buddies who enthusiastically paid tribute to him at the ceremony, like Larry David, Eric Idle, Diane Keaton, Paul Simon (again—what he won't do for a free meal), Queen Latifah, Randy Newman, Tom Hanks, and Martin Short. We also got the chance to have three recent recipients of the Mark Twain Prize in attendance: Carl Reiner, Lily Tomlin, and Lorne Michaels.

Tom Hanks said that Martin "redefined comedy by defining the moment of our ascendancy as a generation. As did Charlie Chaplin, as did the Marx Brothers, as did Laurel and Hardy define their own times, Steve Martin defined ours." Lily Tomlin was no less laudatory, declaring that Martin's "artistry soars to heights of sublime silliness and divine absurdity."

Then came Larry David, a man notoriously difficult to impress—in comedy and life in general. He himself opened his remarks by asking, "What do these people have against Steve Martin that they would even ask me to do this? I'm the last guy you want to do something like this." He then spent the majority of his time telling obviously fake stories meant to make Steve look like a monster—insulting a homeless person, refusing to save a cat, plagiarizing a Dorothy Parker piece for *The New Yorker*, and drunkenly making antisemitic comments toward Larry in public. Larry bookended his insults with apologies and repeated worries that he was ruining the night.

"[Steve] reached into his pocket, took out a flask, and started guzzling some bourbon. I said, 'Steve, what are you doing? You can't do that here. Are you crazy?' He said 'Ahh, shut up, you dirty Jew.' [Pause for uproarious laughter.] Okay, I'm sorry, I'm not a violent person, but I wasn't gonna stand there and let some mean selfish plagiarizing incontinent cowardly drunken egomaniac attack my heritage! So I popped him."

But even Larry David could not help but take a brief moment to be earnest about what Steve Martin meant to him, calling him a "comedy legend" and "one of my idols," before getting right back to slandering his name for laughs.

Finally, Steve Martin took to the stage and was unsurprisingly hilarious. A falsely humble, self-aggrandizing, pretentious acceptance speech felt like the role he was born to play (ironically, of course).

He called the Mark Twain Prize "the only significant American award for comedy except for money." He acknowledged the prestige of his fellow Twain Prize recipients, saying, "When I look at the list of people who have been given this award, it makes me very, very satisfied. But when I look at the list of people who *haven't* been given this award, it makes me even *more* satisfied." Then, he read a quote that he attributed to Mark Twain: "Whatever you do, for God's sake, do not name a prize after me." He closed out the night, as has become his signature, by rocking out on the banjo.

My experience with Steve was that he was nothing but sweet, not to mention hysterical and brilliant onstage and off. As I have gone on to do every year, I emceed the rehearsal dinner (that year it was at the Renwick Gallery), and at one point, Twain Prize–winner Carl Reiner, whom I asked to give that night's final toast to Steve, challenged him: "Steve, you're a big art collector and you think you're so smart. Who painted that?" And one by one, Carl followed Steve all around the room as he guessed the names of the artists for each painting. The curator of the gallery was there with us and confirmed that Steve had gotten almost all of them right. And for the few he didn't, he made educated guesses that were close.

At the end of the dinner, we the executive producers of the Mark Twain Prize invited Steve up to accept a top-of-the-line banjo as a token of gratitude for his life's work. And as we hoped, he then used it to play everyone a few songs.

Steve Martin never stopped amazing me with his quick wit, extraordinary talent, and breadth of knowledge, and it was a pleasure to award him the eighth Mark Twain Prize.

✦ ✦ ✦

In 2006, we gave the Mark Twain Prize to Neil Simon, one of the most prolific and successful American playwrights of our time. He, along with Lorne Michaels, was one of the only honorees who was primarily known for his work *behind* the camera, or away from a camera entirely.

Some people have criticized the Mark Twain Prize in the years when we select younger honorees in the height of their careers, leaving some to wonder whether Mark Twain himself would be selected for the prize today. Those critics need not look any further than Neil Simon for a Twain Prize recipient who fits the mold of Samuel Clemens. They were both chiefly writers, not performers; their best-known works had come decades before 2006; and neither of them were ever cast members or guests on *Saturday Night Live*, albeit for very different reasons.

(Also, in response to the question of whether Mark Twain could win the prize today: it would be difficult to organize, considering that he's been dead for over a century.)

Although Simon never worked on *Saturday Night Live,* he did start his career writing for one of its major predecessors in the 1950s: Sid Caesar's *Your Show of Shows*, working alongside all-time greats like Mel Brooks and Carl Reiner. This kicked off a run of jobs that Simon held writing comedy for television, including *Caesar's Hour* and *The Phil Silvers Show*, before penning his Broadway debut in 1961. *Come Blow Your Horn* was a coming-of-age story that would be the first of several dozen plays and musicals that Simon would write or contribute to, including *Barefoot in the Park*, *The Odd Couple*, and *Promises, Promises*, among so many others. Simon also became an accomplished screenwriter, in part because about two dozen of his plays were adapted into movies. Even if Simon himself wasn't the most visible comedy legend we'd ever honored, his body of work was far-reaching and undeniable—making him the climate change of humorists.

Here's another way that Neil Simon followed in the footsteps of Mark Twain: his work was just as socially relevant as it was funny. His plays and movies explored the reality of middle-class people struggling to survive city life. He used his personal experience to tell stories that made tiny, relatable observations and asked big, meaningful questions.

For Neil Simon's ceremony, we gathered a cast of speakers who represented Simon's influential reach across theater, film, and television, including Christina Applegate, Patricia Heaton, Lucie Arnaz, Nathan Lane, Jason Alexander, Robert Redford, Richard Dreyfuss, and Matthew Broderick. A recurring theme at the ceremony was that these fantastic actors had all reached breakthroughs at key moments in their careers thanks to Simon.

Richard Dreyfuss, who won the Academy Award for Best Actor for his role in *The Goodbye Girl*, said, "He allowed me my whole professional life. He got me right."

And Matthew Broderick, who played Eugene in the original Broadway production of *Brighton Beach Memoirs*, paraphrased a line from that play when he told Simon, "Thank you for making it possible to purchase a small golden palace in the Himalayas."

Carl Reiner, who gave a video tribute, was the one speaker who expressed the opposite sentiment—as a joke. In the early 1960s, Reiner turned down the lead in Simon's first play, *Come Blow Your Horn*. In the video, Reiner reflected on what could have been: "If I had been in your show, I might still be on Broadway, scrounging for work."

For his part, Simon was humble and even came off a bit nervous in his acceptance speech. He talked about how it took him six years to write *Come Blow Your Horn*, named for a nursery rhyme in one of his daughter's books. He called it "a so-so play" that became a "so-so movie." The one success he would admit was how lucrative his career became after that play, reflecting, "For the first time, I had money in the bank. Yes sir, yes sir, three bags full."

✦ ✦ ✦

The tenth year we awarded the Mark Twain Prize was in 2007, which meant that—just barely—we had hosted the ceremony more times than Billy Crystal had hosted the Academy Awards. (It would take us another ten years to pass Bob Hope, who hosted the Oscars nineteen times.)

Billy Crystal, who by then had hosted the Oscars eight times, the Grammys three times, and appeared on the *Comic Relief* charity telecast eight times, was in many ways long overdue for an honor like the Mark Twain Prize. For once, he deserved to *attend* an award ceremony in his honor instead of hosting it in someone else's honor.

He had decades of comedic success under his belt, from his early days as a stand-up in New York City to his role playing Jodie Dallas on *Soap*, one of TV's first openly gay characters, to his tenure as host and cast member on *Saturday Night Live* in the 1980s, to his roles in dozens of films like *When Harry Met Sally*, *City Slickers*, and *Analyze This*. He had just hosted the Oscars again in 2004 and had won a Tony for his autobiographical show, *700 Sundays*, in 2005.

We held that year's rehearsal dinner at the Supreme Court, which lent it a particular air of class and distinction. Obviously, you can't just hold any event at the Supreme Court; you need one of the justices to host you, and we were fortunate enough to have Anthony Kennedy do the honors and grace the evening with his presence.

Speaking of gravitas, the people who showed up to honor Billy Crystal at the ceremony the next day were superstars of comedy, TV, and film, young and old: Barbara Walters, John Goodman, Martin Short, Jimmy Fallon, Bob Costas, Danny DeVito, Rob Reiner, Jon Lovitz, Robert De Niro, and Robin Williams. Perhaps more than any other year up to that point, it was an evening jam-packed with A-list entertainers—and Jon Lovitz.

On the red carpet, Rob Reiner described how Billy Crystal went the extra mile: "He's an amazing guy for a stand-up. I've known a lot of stand-ups in my time. Most of them are very self-involved…. He's unusual in that he's a real family man, and he's very generous with his spirit and his time. Very unusual for a stand-up comedian."

In response, Jon Lovitz quipped: "What are you talkin' about? 'Cause I'm doing stand-up now, and I wasn't listening."

During the show, Robin Williams gave a particularly funny and touching tribute, referencing the waning days of the George W. Bush administration: "Tonight, the audience is filled with luminaries, dignitaries, and power brokers, who are all under the spell of Mister William Crystal. Some of you are also under indictment; you know who you are. So we ask you, please, to turn off your cell phones and your ankle bracelets. Enjoy the evening."

When Billy Crystal came on stage to accept the award, he expressed gratitude that it wasn't posthumous. He joked, "Does this mean I have to retire now? Usually when someone is given an evening like this, they're way too dead to say thank you."

We were very fortunate to get the chance to pay tribute to Steve Martin, Neil Simon, and Billy Crystal while they were still around to appreciate it. We wouldn't always get that lucky.

CHAPTER TWENTY

Tragedy After Tragedy in Comedy

In 2008, after a decade of awarding the Mark Twain Prize, we sought to honor a giant of comedy who was notorious for rejecting the notion of awards, pomp, and circumstance. A lot of times, when people reject the concept of awards, it's only because they weren't good enough to win any. That was obviously not the case with this guy.

In spite of his fraught relationship with acclaim, George Carlin graciously accepted when we asked him to be the eleventh recipient of the Mark Twain Prize.

Carlin was the definitive example of a comedian who did more than make people laugh. He was an artist who was constantly evolving and innovating the form of stand-up comedy. He began in the early 1960s as a clean-cut performer in a suit making lighthearted observational humor, but it didn't take long for him to become a long-haired iconoclast who questioned and mocked every sacred institution imaginable. His first Grammy Award–winning album, 1972's *FM & AM*, made this transformation official, featuring both his early material and his taboo jokes on opposing sides of the record.

He was one of the most prolific stand-up comedians of all time, having released an eye-popping fourteen comedy specials on HBO, in addition to three *New York Times* bestselling books, twenty-two albums, a plethora of appearances in TV and film, and countless hours on the road performing for rapturous crowds of dedicated fans. He was the first person ever to host *Saturday Night Live* in 1975, and he had appeared on *The Tonight Show* over 130 times starting in 1966. Oh, and he was still going: he had just released his latest HBO special and album, *It's Bad for Ya*, in March of that year.

We sent out a press release on June 17, 2008, proudly announcing our selection, and George replied publicly with, "Thank you, Mister Twain. Have your people call my people." We were all set to put up a wonderful show honoring the man who gave us classic bits like "Seven Words You Can Never Say on Television," "A Place for My Stuff," and "Modern Man."

But just five days later, George Carlin died as a result of heart failure in Santa Monica at the age of seventy-one. After he died, the outpouring of love and support for him and his body of work was overwhelming. Jerry Seinfeld wrote an obituary for him in the *New York Times,* praising Carlin's role as a pioneer in the industry: "[W] hen I reach my own end, whatever tumbling cataclysmic vortex of existence I'm spinning through, in that moment I will still have to think, 'Carlin already did it.'"

And Joan Rivers wrote one for the *New York Post*: "He was so head and shoulders ahead of everybody. He wasn't sentimental, but don't kid yourself—he would have loved all the attention he's getting right now. Just don't say that he 'passed away.' 'Passed to where?' he would ask."

We had never given the Mark Twain Prize posthumously, but with Carlin's legacy being cherished so passionately in the days and weeks after his death, it was clearer than ever that he was the right choice to receive that year's honor. And it seemed somehow fitting that a man who disdained award ceremonies would sooner skip out on earth than participate in a self-congratulating tribute to himself.

We had no trouble whatsoever getting his talented friends and protégés to gather and pay tribute to his legacy. His influence extended to so many generations of comics, as the night's stacked lineup made clear: we had Richard Belzer, Lewis Black, Margaret Cho, Denis Leary, Bill Maher, Joan Rivers, Garry Shandling, Jon Stewart, and Lily Tomlin.

And in lieu of having Carlin there in person, we sifted through the enormous wealth of archival footage of his recorded performances and found highlights from every era of his career: from the clean-cut, suit-wearing, traditional standup on *The Hollywood Palace* with host Jimmy Durante; to the unshaven, long-haired iconoclast who performed a set mocking a cardboard cutout of his old self; to the thoughtful, pony-tailed, elder statesman of comedy worshipped by those who grew up with his albums. We jam-packed the night with as much Carlin as we possibly could without him being physically present.

Bill Maher opened the show, and he pointed out the irony of the formality: "Here was what George Carlin said he wanted by way of a memorial. He said, 'It should be extremely informal.' So here we all are, in dark suits at the Kennedy Center, with lots of people who love golf."

Garry Shandling shared a story about the time during college he drove two hours to see Carlin perform and gave him some unsolicited material, which Carlin read and then sat backstage giving Shandling notes for twenty minutes. Twelve years later, Shandling told that story while presenting Carlin with a lifetime achievement award, and Carlin quipped, "First of all, I'm sorry for encouraging Garry to pursue his career. He's been nothing but a pain in the ass ever since."

Finally, instead of closing out the night with an acceptance speech, we had a beautifully touching performance of one of George Carlin's favorite songs: "Stand by Me," as performed by its original singer, Ben E. King.

George's daughter, Kelly, was in attendance, and she was a wonderfully gracious person to be around for the whole process. Peter

Kaminsky set up a dinner with her and the executive producers at Citronelle, a fantastic restaurant owned by Michel Richard. Michel served us personally, in an experience made all the better by Kelly's excitement about the show. She said George would have loved it, which was the greatest honor that we could have received.

Another honor—at a distant second—came the following year, when, for the first time, the Mark Twain Prize received an Emmy nomination for Outstanding Special Class Program.

We took out an ad in a magazine to campaign for George to get his due, and it read, "It's the seven words George Carlin never got to say on television: 'Thank you all for this wonderful Emmy.'" Kelly Carlin nixed my original draft, which was "Thank you all for this f**king Emmy." But you get the idea.

In the end, we lost to the Beijing 2008 Olympic Games Opening Ceremony. Really? How much work could it possibly be to set up some cameras and carry a torch around? I'm not saying I'm still bitter, but I haven't had Chinese food since. Obviously, the night was about Carlin, not us, but it would have been nice to add an Emmy to his stuff.

✦   ✦   ✦

The next year, we faced a different sort of tragedy in awarding the Mark Twain Prize. In 2008, George Carlin couldn't be there; in 2009, Bill Cosby *was* there.

When we offered Bill Cosby the Mark Twain Prize, we had no idea about all of the heinous, unforgivable things he had done to women over the course of his career. Of course, we would never have given him that honor if we had known about the more than fifty women who would eventually accuse him of sexual misconduct, assault, and rape.

In fact, in 2018, after Cosby was found guilty of indecent aggravated assault, the Kennedy Center made the unprecedented move of rescinding his Kennedy Center Honors and his Mark Twain Prize. We held off on making that decision through all the reporting and news cycles leading up to his trial because we wanted to stick by the principle that people are "innocent until proven guilty." When he was proven guilty, his accolades went.

I'm proud we made that decision. Some people believe you should separate the art from the artist, but the Mark Twain Prize celebrates the art *and* the artist, and so much of Cosby's work was tied to the family-friendly persona he presented to the public. We couldn't remain silent. If Mr. Rogers killed a guy, I'd want his awards taken away too.

You might imagine that because we didn't know what he had done, we were blissfully unaware and had a great time backstage with Bill Cosby, who carried the same gravitas and humility as the decade of Mark Twain Prize recipients who preceded him.

But you'd be imagining wrong. In addition to being a sex criminal, Bill Cosby was a complete asshole. I'm not joking. It's been said that you can tell a lot about a person by how they treat people who have nothing to offer them in return. By that measure, maybe we should have seen Cosby's horrific behavior as part of a larger horrific package.

Cosby showed some true colors at the rehearsal dinner, at which he was condescending and rude to the waitstaff. He barked orders at the show's production people too—basically, he blatantly disregarded anyone whom he did not perceive to be on his level in terms of fame or power.

Cosby's self-centered nature even hurt the ceremony itself. When the man himself took the stage, he dragged on…and on….and on. The Mark Twain Prize recipient is expected to give five, maybe seven minutes of remarks to close out the evening. Cosby got up there and he rambled and ad-libbed for over half an hour. It got to the point where, toward the end, Cosby got a big laugh when he said, "This honor tonight is wonderful. That's why I'm taking my time to thank everybody who came to support me." I don't think he was joking, but it was almost inconceivable that he could take even more time than he already had. Eventually, he managed to get off the stage before we had to start setting up for the 2010 Mark Twain Prize.

By the way, on top of everything else, Cosby had refused our offers to give him the Mark Twain Prize for *years* because—of all reasons—he didn't approve of the vulgarity of our very first ceremony honoring Richard Pryor. Ironic considering he was, to his core, an arrogant, two-faced, hypocritical person who abused his power for selfish ends time and time again. But hey, at least he didn't cuss in public.

CHAPTER TWENTY-ONE

Twain in the Tweens

After Tom Daschle lost his reelection bid in 2004, suddenly a bunch of talented, hardworking staffers for one of the most high-level Democrats in the country were left adrift. Then, as the 2008 presidential race revved up, and Daschle endorsed then-Senator Obama's insurgent candidacy, a bunch of Daschle's people made the transition to the campaign—and eventually, the White House. Perhaps the most high-profile Daschle alum in Obama's orbit was Pete Rouse, who was Senator Daschle's chief of staff, then the chief of staff for Obama for America, before taking on the role of senior adviser to the president after the 2008 election.

What the Obama folks might not have understood is that when you adopt Tom Daschle's people, you get me too.[8] I sat on the National Finance Committee for the Obama campaign, and early in Obama's presidency, I called Pete Rouse and let him know I was interested in being appointed to the board of the Kennedy Center because I wanted to be as involved with the Mark Twain Prize as possible. Pete put in a good word, and in 2011, I became one of only two people in the Kennedy Center's history up to that point to get appointed to its board by two different presidents of the United States. Or you could

---

8 I'm like complimentary chips and salsa. And as we can all agree—that's often the best part of the meal.

say I snuck in under the nose of two different presidents—however you want to put it.

Around that time, after many years of honoring living legends who had made their mark decades earlier, there was a period when we shifted to paying tribute to comedians who were firmly in their prime. This wasn't a conscious decision per se, but early in the development of the Mark Twain Prize we decided that it would *not* necessarily be a lifetime achievement award—at least in the sense that it doesn't have to be awarded at the end of a career. Instead, it's meant to honor anyone who has achieved the highest degree of excellence and influence in comedy, regardless of what age they achieved it. Whether you're ninety-three or thirty-nine, the key question is: Has your career changed the shape of American comedy?

In that regard, the next three recipients of the Mark Twain Prize fit the bill: Tina Fey, Will Ferrell, and Ellen DeGeneres.

In 2010, Tina Fey became our thirteenth recipient. She was the third woman to receive the Mark Twain Prize, as well as the youngest winner ever at the age of forty. But despite her relative youth, Tina's career was unmatched in many regards: she had been *Saturday Night Live's* first female head writer, one of that show's all-time most iconic cast members, the screenwriter behind a modern comedy classic in *Mean Girls,* the creator and star of one of the best sitcoms of the 2000s in *30 Rock,* and she did a Sarah Palin impression that was so uncanny and biting that it might have handed Barack Obama the 2008 election—it was either that or the financial crisis. I go back and forth.

Everything you might imagine about Tina Fey's personality based on her charming public persona is true; and in fact, she exceeds expectations. She's not just hilarious—she's lightning quick. She's not just self-deprecating—she is genuinely humble. She doesn't just project relatability—she makes you feel like a close friend with every greeting and side comment. That was true when she was my dinner partner for Carol Burnett's rehearsal dinner, and that was true when Tina was the honoree herself.

Thanks to then-House Speaker Nancy Pelosi, we had that year's rehearsal dinner in the National Statuary Hall, a chamber of the Capitol that displays statues of accomplished Americans representing each state. During my opening remarks as emcee of the dinner, I said that she was the most powerful Speaker since Sam Rayburn, the longest-serving Speaker ever and a mentor to Lyndon B. Johnson. Actually, "powerful" is probably an understatement.

Then, I got to explain the reasons why we chose Tina Fey for that year's prize: "There are many reasons we're honoring Tina Fey this year. I want to mention two of them. First, Mark Twain was a lover of satire and a believer that our country would always produce people worthy of satire. As Twain called them, 'Toadstools who thought they were truffles.' Today, we call them politicians. Second, the one nobody has admitted—until now—is that *Tina is Emmy bait.*" (Unfortunately, our ploy didn't work: we did not get nominated for the Tina Fey ceremony.)

There was just one bizarre moment that night. A bunch of other speakers from the ceremony also gave remarks at the rehearsal dinner, including Steve Martin, Betty White, and Jon Hamm. But when Lorne Michaels started to approach the microphone he suddenly stopped, turned around, and sat back down.

I never figured out why he decided to back out of giving a toast, but I ended up taking a page from *SNL* and threw to a break: "We'll be right back with more toasts!" And then I went over to Janie's dinner partner—this guy Steve Martin—and asked him if he could go up next. He graciously agreed, delivered his toast from the table, and the rest of the night went on without a hitch.

I don't begrudge Lorne. After all, could you really pay tribute to an *SNL* star without something going wrong live on stage?

✦ ✦ ✦

The next day's ceremony featured Fred Armisen, Jimmy Fallon, Seth Meyers, Amy Poehler, Tracy Morgan, Jane Krakowski, Jon Hamm, Steve Carell, Steve Martin, and Betty White. Lorne Michaels also showed up and actually went through with giving his remarks this time. Plus, Jennifer Hudson belted a powerful rendition of Aretha Franklin's "Respect" in Tina's honor.

Steve Martin kicked off the night with a wonderfully sarcastic dig at how "the Mark Twain Prize has become a degraded and worthless award that brings the recipient such shame and dishonor." Then he addressed criticism of that year's choice of honoree: "Some have suggested that Tina is too young to be given a lifetime achievement award. But you wouldn't say that if you knew that Tina only has two more hours left to live."

Later, Amy Poehler, Tina's close friend and longtime comedy partner, also invoked Twain(s): "Mark Twain once said, 'Against the assault of laughter, nothing can stand.' But it was Shania Twain who said, 'Man! I Feel Like a Woman!'"

Finally, Tina Fey took the stage and gave an acceptance speech, thanking her pals by noting that she realized that they were "all very busy people with families, and it means so much to me to know that you care more about show business than you do about them."

She emphasized her family's impact on her career: "I want to thank my family. They say that funny people often come from a difficult childhood or a troubled family, so to my family I say...they're giving me the Mark Twain Prize for American Humor. What did you animals do to me?"

And she also dinged Twain himself: "I hope that like Mark Twain, one hundred years from now people will see my work, and think, 'Wow, that is actually pretty racist.'"

✦ ✦ ✦

Another modern *SNL* great received the fourteenth Mark Twain Prize in 2011: Will Ferrell. By the mid-2000s, Will Ferrell was one of the most popular comedic actors in the world. A golden boy of the legendary "Frat Pack"—a group of funny actors who came up together and which included Jack Black, Steve Carell, Ben Stiller, Vince Vaughn, and Owen Wilson—Will was the lead in hit after hit after hit. From raunchy comedies like *Old School* to family classics like *Elf* to high-concept, character-driven movies like *Anchorman* and *Talladega Nights*, Will Ferrell consistently demonstrated a magic touch: he could make anything funnier. It's a tall order to do a George W. Bush impression that's funnier than real life, but Will somehow managed it.

That was also what made him, in my view, one of the best *SNL* cast members of all time. He could take the dumbest, most intellectually bankrupt idea—lovers in a hot tub, overgrown cheerleaders, a rogue cowbell player—and, by sheer brute force of raw comedic ability (and an impenetrable stare into the camera), make it one of the funniest sketches you've ever seen.

He also started his own comedy empire in Funny or Die, which I touched upon in my remarks at his rehearsal dinner at the National Archives: "Will Ferrell's career has been about more than cracking jokes. By founding the website Funny or Die, he has helped change the way comedy is done. Funny or die. Will, if those are the only two choices, you just might live forever."

A few months prior, I had attended a Kennedy Center board meeting with Jacqueline Mars of the Mars candy company. She had just made a generous gift coinciding with the Washington National Opera's merging into the Kennedy Center. She is an incredibly kind person and a truly giving philanthropist, but the reason I'm bringing her up is because of her unrivaled access to custom M&Ms.

A friend of mine had gotten me some custom M&Ms with my face on them for one of my birthdays, and it was so funny and ridiculous, I knew that it would be a great party favor for the Twain rehearsal dinner. After the meeting, I went up to Jacqueline and asked if there was any chance she could get us some M&Ms with Will Ferrell's face on them for the dinner. The only question she asked me was, "What color?" They ended up being a huge hit, so much so that Will wandered around the National Archives asking if he could take all the M&Ms home with him.

I also got the chance to take Will Ferrell to meet President Obama and tour the White House. When I brought Will down to the Situation Room, the young White House staffers got excited and stood up to greet him, causing Will to beg them to sit down. "Hey! I don't want the world to go to hell because you guys aren't paying attention to what you're doing."

Will's Mark Twain Prize ceremony featured Ed Asner, Adam McKay, Conan O'Brien, Molly Shannon, Jack Black, Matthew Broderick, and Paul Rudd. Jack Black burst onto the stage to open the show with a rendition of "We Will Rock You" that, to use his terminology, would have to be described as face-meltingly delicious. In his parody, he tweaked the lyrics a little bit to match the evening's subject:

Ferrell is a boy
Make a big noise
Playin' in the street
Gonna win the Mark Twain someday!
Ya got mud on your face
You're not a disgrace
In fact: you are the opposite of a disgrace!

Will will, Will will, rock you!
Will will, Will will, rock you!

Will Ferrell himself was responsible that night for what was one of the funniest moments in the history of the Mark Twain Prize ceremony.

He got onto the stage, accepted a standing ovation, cradled the Twain prize, and before his intro music was even done playing, he dropped the bust of Twain onto the stage and it immediately shattered. The music faltered, and as the applause died down and the sound of confusion echoed throughout the room, Will pathetically attempted to piece the prize back together—which, in effect, was just perching Twain's cracked face atop a pile of rubble. That would've been funny enough on his own, but Will stretched out the gag with his opening lines:

"As I stare at this magnificent bust of Mark Twain…I'm reminded of how humbled I am to receive such an honor, and how I vow to take very special care of it.[9] I will never let it out of my sight. I will find a place of honor in my house for this magnificent bust. If my children try to touch it, or even look at it, I will beat them. It means that much to me. In fact, I told my wife that maybe I should buy it its own seat for the plane ride home."

It was such an authentic moment of physical comedy; I'm sure there were plenty of people in the room who couldn't tell if it was a joke or not. (Of course, Will had cleared the bit with us beforehand, and the bust he broke was a fake. We actually made about fifteen different faux Twain plasters, one of which is in my home.)

Will went on to give a characteristically hilarious speech, with lines addressing what a humbling moment it was for him: "I am the fourteenth recipient of the Mark Twain Prize. You're probably asking yourself, 'Why did it take so long?' Well for thirteen consecutive years, I have been begged by the Kennedy Center to accept this award, and for thirteen consecutive years, I have emphatically said no."

9   It's basically a mound of dust with a mustache at this point.

And he also commented on the nonhistoric nature of his win: "I have just been informed that I am only the eleventh Caucasian to receive this prestigious award."

At the end of his speech, we got a rare glimpse at Will being totally sincere: "I want to thank the Kennedy Center for being one of the few places that upholds comedy as what it truly is: an art form. Thank you, and goodnight."

President Barack Obama greets Will Ferrell and his wife, Viveca Paulin, in the Oval Office.

✦ ✦ ✦

Many of the Mark Twain Prize's honorees have cut their teeth in the world of late-night comedy—whether as character performers, writers, standups, or guests—but in 2012, the fifteenth Mark Twain Prize went to a comedian who, in addition to her work as a standup and sitcom star, reinvented the daytime talk show: Ellen DeGeneres.

Ellen has had one of the most groundbreaking yet challenging careers of any comedian out there. Throughout the 1980s, she honed her skills as a standup, and in 1986 she accomplished the first of many history-making television moments by being the first woman ever to be invited to sit on Johnny Carson's couch after performing a standup set on *The Tonight Show*. She continued to make film and TV appearances into the 1990s, before starring in her own sitcom, *Ellen*, on ABC starting in 1994.

Then, in 1997, as I mentioned while talking about our tribute to Lily Tomlin, Ellen came out as a lesbian, both in real life and in-character on her show, making her show the first with an openly gay character in the lead. Within a year, *Ellen* was canceled, and as she would reveal later on, Ellen DeGeneres dealt with depression and isolation in the months and years that followed. At that moment, Ellen's choice to be honest about her identity had ground her career to a halt.

Until it didn't. Because starting in 2003, when Ellen got a chance to host the daytime talk show *The Ellen DeGeneres Show*, she put her true self front and center despite continued pushback from TV executives, and the show was an immediate success that has only grown in influence in the decades since.

By the time we selected her to receive the Mark Twain Prize in 2012, *The Ellen DeGeneres Show* had been on the air for nearly a decade, and—to give you an idea of just how much the media landscape had changed in a short time—Ellen had just hit ten million Twitter followers, making her the most-followed comedian in the world and one of the most popular celebrities online, period. In endearing herself to the world through humor, she became one of the first gay people that many of her fans saw on TV. Ellen is not just "one of the most successful queer comedians" or "one of the most successful female comedians," but one of the most successful comedians altogether.

We held that year's rehearsal dinner in the Benjamin Franklin Room at the State Department—the same venue where the Kennedy Center Honors typically holds its rehearsal dinner.

Among others, I got to introduce Jason Mraz as "a man whose name is desperately in need of one additional vowel." I got to call out the emcee chops of Steve Harvey, joking that "he'll probably be hosting this before the night is over." And I got to share some pertinent information with Broadway star Kristin Chenoweth: "Kristin, for what it's worth, I yodel."

But most importantly, I got to pay tribute to the woman of the hour, Ellen DeGeneres. Here's what I said about her impact on this country, which I still believe now: "When the 2001 Emmys were delayed for seven weeks as a result of the September Eleventh attacks, it was Ellen who hosted the rescheduled event…and gave us permission to laugh again. I can't say it better than she did: 'What would bug the Taliban more than seeing a gay woman in a suit surrounded by Jews?'"

Because Ellen and her show were so popular, we had no trouble getting a wide variety of amazing guests from across the spectrum of entertainment to pay tribute at the ceremony, including Kristen Chenoweth, Steve Harvey, Sean Hayes, Jimmy Kimmel, John Krasinski, John Leguizamo, Jane Lynch, Jason Mraz, and of course, Lily Tomlin.

Ellen's fellow talk show luminary, Kimmel, started the night strong with a laugh line right out of the gate: "As you know, we are here tonight to say goodbye to our friend Ellen DeGeneres."

He then went on to emphasize how inspiring Ellen was to him, saying "because of Ellen…in 1998, I mustered the courage to come out of the closet despite the fact that I'm not gay."

When Ellen accepted the prize, she was as hilarious as ever. With the 2012 election between President Obama and Mitt Romney just days away, she alluded to public broadcasting's precarious position: "Thanks to everyone at PBS. I am so happy to be a part of your farewell season."

She talked about the journey it took for her to finally realize she needed to be a comedian: "I tried everything. I shucked oysters; I painted houses; I sold vacuum cleaners; I was a court runner; but there was always a voice saying, 'You should be doing something different,' and it was usually my boss and I was being fired."

And finally, she closed out the night by quoting the Taylor Swift song "Ours," and falsely attributing the line to Mark Twain—thereby paying tribute not just to Twain, but to the rich history of making stuff up and claiming he said it.

ELLEN DeGENERES

CAPPY—
YOU ARE KIND AND
VERY FUNNY— THANKS
FOR ALL OF IT. WHAT A
NIGHT!

CHAPTER TWENTY-TWO

The One That Got Away

There are a few people who have not accepted the Mark Twain Prize when we've offered it to them, for various reasons. As I've already mentioned, we had to ask Cosby a few times before he agreed to be honored—in retrospect, maybe we should've permitted him to decline. We also asked Robin Williams on a couple of occasions before he passed away, and he certainly deserved it; there's no question he's on my personal Mount Rushmore of comedy.

But one honoree who has been out of our reach for decades stands out to me, because he's an all-time great—a master of comedy as an actor, writer, and director—and that's Mel Brooks. (I'd call him our "white whale," but that's a reference for the Herman Melville Prize.)

The case for Mel Brooks receiving the Mark Twain Prize is so obvious that it feels ridiculous to have to spell it out. He helped to revolutionize TV comedy as a writer for *Your Show of Shows* and *Get Smart*. Then he wrote and directed a bunch of classic movies, which earned him his status as possibly the greatest comedy auteur of all time, including *The Producers*; *Blazing Saddles*; *Young Frankenstein*; *History of the World, Part 1*; and *Spaceballs*. Like Whoopi Goldberg, he is part of the incredibly exclusive club of people to have won an Emmy, Grammy, Oscar, and Tony Award. And he has made countless cameo appearances and voice acting roles in movies and TV, many of which are as himself in the role of entertainment legend.

It may seem like a disgrace that he has never received the Mark Twain Prize. In fact, doesn't it seem like he should have been one of the first? But the truth is that it hasn't been for a lack of trying. We've formally offered him the prize on at least three occasions, and he's always turned it down. We even recruited his longtime friend and Twain Prize–winner, Carl Reiner, to twist his arm and get him on board, but it never worked.

Meanwhile, in 2009, he *did* accept an invitation to receive the Kennedy Center Honors, alongside Dave Brubeck, Grace Bumbry, Robert De Niro, and Bruce Springsteen. So it's not like he doesn't go to awards ceremonies, nor is he allergic to the drywall in the Kennedy Center.

Not being able to give Mel Brooks the Mark Twain Prize is disappointing on a number of levels. For one thing, it means that so many young people who grew up after Mel Brooks's heyday may not get the chance to see his legacy honored while he's still around. Hell, a whole generation of people have come of age just since we started the Mark Twain Prize. For another, half the reason I wanted to honor Mel Brooks was so I could meet the guy myself!

At the very least, the latter problem has since been resolved. In early 2016, I got a call from Deborah Rutter, the president of the Kennedy Center, and she told me that Mel Brooks was coming to the Kennedy Center to give a talk after a screening of *Blazing Saddles*. (I didn't try to pitch a mid-evening quick-and-dirty Mark Twain Prize ceremony for him, but maybe I should have.) Deborah invited me to come to the show and join Mel for dinner in the Green Room beforehand. We were also joined by Kennedy Center chairman David Rubenstein.

I was fascinated by the catering laid out according to his rider. Once someone gets past ninety and is still vibrant and active, you have to wonder what magic diet fuels their eternal youth. For Mel, it seemed to be egg salad sandwiches, Lay's potato chips, a package of Oreo cookies, and Coca-Cola. Real Coke! Not Diet or Coke Zero. For a nonagenarian, that's basically crack. Nevertheless, Mel came in, alive and well.

I'm supposed to keep it cool in these situations, but I was a bit intimidated to meet Mel Brooks; there's something extra special about seeing a guy in the flesh whom you grew up idolizing on TV and movies.

Mel ripped into the egg salad sandwiches, and in his fervor he ended up spilling egg salad on his dark blue suit coat. "Cappy," he asked, "could you flick the egg salad off my coat?"

I'm no scientist, but I know enough about physics to understand that one cannot "flick" egg salad off a coat. Egg salad does not flick; it smears. But when Mel Brooks asks you to do the impossible, you'd damn well better try. Long story short, I smeared egg salad all over his coat.

Despite the baseless smear, now that I was face-to-face with Mel, I decided to make a last-ditch effort on the big ask. "Please accept the Mark Twain Prize," I pleaded. "We've asked you several times!"

"I just don't know about it," he said. "I've been reluctant to do it, but I'll think about it."

I said: "You know, Mel, if you don't do it, we're just going to have to do a Number Six."

That reference to one of the raunchiest moments in *Blazing Saddles* got a big laugh from him—for me, a bigger coup than him accepting the Mark Twain Prize anyway.

The four of us in the room got together for a picture, and on his way out to the stage, Mel said, "I'll get back to you soon about the Mark Twain Prize." Which was true. His guy got back to us a couple weeks later and told us "he's not going to be able to take it." He still hasn't—and has never told us why.

As of writing, the man is ninety-five years old. Maybe his best years are still ahead of him; who knows. But even if his Mark Twain Prize ceremony never happens, let me go on the record and say, Mel Brooks has earned it many times over.

Here's an idea for a posthumous show: let's give Mark Twain the Mel Brooks Prize.

Cappy McGarr poses with Mel Brooks. Or is it the other way around?

CHAPTER TWENTY-THREE

Carol Burnett and the Car Boy

In 2013 and 2014, we honored a pair of comedians who hosted iconic hit network TV shows. She dominated the world of sketch; he is regarded as a legendary joke-teller. The sixteenth and seventeenth recipients of the Mark Twain Prize were Carol Burnett and Jay Leno.

Carol Burnett made her TV debut in 1955 in a minor guest role on *The Paul Winchell Show*. Over the course of the next decade, she made a bunch of one-off appearances on shows, specials, and TV movies, until her star grew enough to sign a ten-year contract with CBS. That contract allowed her the option to put up thirty hour-long episodes of a variety show at a time of her choosing, and that became the now-iconic sketch program *The Carol Burnett Show*, which itself ran for eleven seasons and nearly three hundred episodes.

After that, she appeared in all kinds of TV shows and plays and movies, like *Annie*, *Love Letters*, and *All My Children*; sometimes she would play outrageous characters, and sometimes playing herself provided more than enough star power. But no matter the role, she was always one of the most committed, hysterical actors in Hollywood, period.

The year that Carol Burnett won the Mark Twain Prize was particularly special—when President Obama showed her around the Oval Office, it was clear to me that he had a deeply held admiration for her, the sort of reverence you can only have for someone whom you've idolized since your formative years. He told her that he was a huge fan, that his family loved *The Carol Burnett Show*, that Michelle's family loved *The Carol Burnett Show*, and how much her work meant to him growing up and throughout his life.

The night before the show, we had our traditional rehearsal dinner at the Folger Shakespeare Library on Capitol Hill, and I started my opening remarks as emcee accordingly: "We are honored to be here at the Folger Shakespeare Library. William Shakespeare wrote that some men achieve greatness and others have greatness thrust upon them, which makes greatness sound a lot like Obamacare."

Then I turned to paying tribute to the woman of the hour: "Carol got her first big break the way many aspiring young actresses do: on a mattress."

Carol knew where the joke was going, and waited for the laughter to die down before she shouted: "Only once!"

That got a huge laugh, of course, but it didn't undermine my punchline: "…But in her case, it was the Broadway show *Once Upon a Mattress*, for which she earned a Tony nomination."

Tina Fey was my dinner partner that night, and when I sat down later, she said: "Mattress joke? Solid." Now *that* was validating. I could tell a thousand bad jokes, and I could still think back to that moment and feel like a rock star.

Then there was a moment that made me feel like a country star: having built some confidence after going back-and-forth with Carol, I ad-libbed a challenge.

"Carol, I know you have a great yodel. I happen to yodel too. So here's what I'll do. If you'll yodel, I'll yodel right back."

Sure enough, she broke out a Tarzan-style yodel, and I responded with a yodel that was clean, crisp, and clear. It was the greatest yodeling duel the Folger Shakespeare Library has ever seen.

The first toaster I introduced at the rehearsal dinner was Carol's longtime friend and co-star, the (now) late, great Tim Conway. After a quick joke—"Tim is a gifted improviser. At least, according to my heavily prepared remarks"—I called him up to the stage.

What followed was a brilliantly absurd set from an all-time comedic genius.

Conway was sitting at the front table, which was literally five feet away from the podium. And in fact, we had told all the toasters that we would bring microphones to them to deliver from their seats. But nevertheless, he stood up, took the microphone, said "Thank you," put the microphone back down, and started walking across the room like he was about to leave. None of us had any idea what he was doing. He climbed up to the balcony—which, by the way, is a gorgeous antique-looking architecture like something out of *Harry Potter*, adding to the bizarre visual—but then he came right back down again, and awkwardly wove in between tables back toward the microphone. At this point, it was clear he was doing a bit, and people started laughing at how ridiculously grandiose his walk to the podium had become. Finally, he got back to the microphone, tapped it, and said: "I have nothing to say."

Explosion of laughter. Then, he started fidgeting and searching his pockets, and said, "Oh wait a minute, I did take notes at church last Sunday on the preacher's sermon…" proceeding to read from a napkin. It was incredible stuff.

The next night at the Kennedy Center, Carol Burnett's far-reaching influence on multiple generations of women in comedy was reflected in the majority-female lineup who paid tribute to her, like Julie Andrews and Vicki Lawrence, as well as younger comedians like Fey, Rashida Jones, Amy Poehler, and Maya Rudolph.

Carol even invited a relative unknown to take the stage: Rosemary Watson, who did an uncanny impression of Hillary Clinton. (In fact, her impersonation is right up there along with those by Amy Poehler,

Kate McKinnon, and Hillary Clinton.) It goes to show how dedicated Carol is to advancing women in comedy: she offered an up-and-coming performer stage time during an evening dedicated to her own legacy. And then we had a few token dudes: Tony Bennett, Tim Conway, Martin Short, and Bruce Vilanch.

The night started with Tina Fey, who, as arguably the foremost sketch comedian of our time, and a former recipient of the Mark Twain Prize, was the perfect person to pass the baton: "We are here tonight to celebrate the hilarious and lovely Carol Burnett. Aside from six Emmys, five Golden Globes, eight People's Choice Awards, and a Peabody, in 2009, Ms. Burnett received a Kennedy Center Honor, and in 2006, the Presidential Medal of Freedom. It really is a testament to her professionalism that she is showing up for this tonight."

Amy Poehler came out in a raggedy wig while walking several dogs, playing "Roz Dozer, Carol Burnett's longtime personal assistant." She thanked Carol for the opportunity: "I was surprised that Carol asked me to speak tonight. I usually stay behind the scenes, but Carol said, 'No, Roz, I want you up there. I want you to stand on stage and publicly apologize for getting my coffee order wrong.'"

Toward the end of the night, the always-classy Tony Bennett sang a nostalgic rendition of "The Way You Look Tonight" for Carol and blew her a kiss.

Finally, Carol Burnett accepted the Mark Twain Prize to a standing ovation. Her opening line was simple, humble, emotional, and funny all at once: "This is very encouraging."

Then came the turn, which poked fun at the previous honorees and the show's setting: "I mean, it was a long time coming, but...I understand because there's so many people funnier than I am...especially here in Washington. But with any luck, they'll soon get voted out, and I'll still have the Mark Twain Prize."

After giving a gracious acceptance speech, in the highlight of the evening, Carol sang a few lines of her classic "Sign Off" song, and pretended to forget the words despite having sung the song thousands of times.

"I'm so glad we had this time together
Just to have a laugh, or…something something something,
Seems we just get started
And before you know it
Comes the time we have to say 'So long.'"

Then she tugged on her ear, and tugged on the Twain bust's ear, and left the stage.

Cappy McGarr, President Barack Obama, Carol Burnett, and Kennedy Center Chairman David Rubenstein stand in the Oval Office with the Mark Twain Prize—and they're so glad they've had this time together.

CAROL BURNETT   10.28.13

Cappy, Dear —
Thank you for one of the most
memorable times of my life!
you are a delight and a
joy to be around.
Gratefully and with love —
Carol

✦ ✦ ✦

The following year, we gave the Mark Twain Prize to Jay Leno. He had just wrapped up his (second) run as host of *The Tonight Show*, which made it as good a time as any to pay tribute to his career. It was also probably the first year we could even weave it into his schedule between *Tonight Show* tapings and road gigs.

As we did for every recipient of the Twain Prize since 2002, we commissioned a stylized caricature of Jay Leno from the amazingly talented artist Robert Risko, whose work has been seen in just about every magazine you can think of, like *Vanity Fair*, *Rolling Stone*, and *The New Yorker*. I bring it up now just because Jay's cartoon was the first to feature a chin that was *smaller* than the original.

From 1992 to 2009, and then again from 2010 to 2014, Jay Leno hosted a *Tonight Show* that was consistently #1 in the ratings. Unlike his predecessor Johnny Carson, Jay only ever had one guest host over the course of his entire tenure—in 2003, he and Katie Couric switched jobs for the day. Her performance was well received, which might explain why Jay never let anyone else sit behind the desk again.

On top of that, he continued to perform live sets all over the country on his "days off." In the years since (in addition to his ongoing vehicle-centric CNBC series *Jay Leno's Garage*) he hasn't quit booking hundreds of shows a year since he retired from *The Tonight Show*.

In that spirit, Jay wasn't available to attend a rehearsal dinner the night before the ceremony; he already had a gig. Instead, we had a rehearsal lunch on the day of the show. Jay had been friends with then-Vice President Joe Biden, so I called a friend of mine (who happened to be Biden's chief of staff), Steve Ricchetti, and we arranged to host the lunch in the vice president's residence at the Naval Observatory. I emceed the afternoon with Leno, Biden, and the second lady all in attendance.

The vice president's presence, as always, was a great opportunity for humor. I addressed him directly while talking about the Mark Twain Prize, saying, "Mister Vice President, I don't think any of us can say it better than you did. This award is a Big Fff...unny Deal."

And we managed to get a dig in on Leno's recent unemployment *and* his scheduling complications: "We usually do a dinner the night before the Twain. But Jay told us, 'I don't do late night anymore.'"

Just like his *Tonight Show*, Leno's Mark Twain Prize ceremony was a well-oiled machine featuring a lot of heavy-duty celebrity talent. We heard from Robert Klein, Jerry Seinfeld, Wanda Sykes, Chelsea Handler, and J. B. Smoove; Garth Brooks, Kristin Chenoweth, and Leno's longtime bandleader, Kevin Eubanks, played. And in a nod to the future of comedy, we heard tributes from a younger generation following in Leno's footsteps, like Al Madrigal, Seth Meyers, and Leno's direct successor as host of *The Tonight Show*, Jimmy Fallon.

Fittingly, it was Fallon who started the night, and he was respectful and deferential to Jay's legacy. That was a big deal, considering the often-contentious nature of late night, which he alluded to: "When

I got the chance to take over *The Tonight Show*, Jay was full of great advice. He told me to make my monologues longer; he said always make my guests look good; he told me to enjoy high-risk activities like jumping school buses with motorcycles, putting my head inside a lion's mouth, something called bungee-less jumping..."

Later, Seth Meyers, Jimmy's successor as the host of NBC's *Late Night*, remarked on Jay's incredible abilities as a relentless joke writer, regardless of politics: "Jay loved good jokes. And with politics, Jay always kept you guessing. Just when the audience thought he supported Democrats, he would tell a joke about Democrats. Before Republicans stopped laughing, he had told a joke about them. Because Jay knew: Republican or Democrat, if you're a politician, you can also be a joke."

Sure enough, when Jay took the stage at the end of the night, he gave one of the most punchline-heavy acceptance speeches the Mark Twain Prize had ever seen. A lot of comedians break from their comedic routines to give a vulnerable, verklempt speech as soon as they have the Twain bust in front of them. But Jay was a joke guy, through and through. For him, it was another chance to deliver a classic ten-minute standup set, right from the first line: "You know, to get ready for this event tonight, I read a lot of Mark Twain. I didn't actually read it; I listened to audio tapes as read by Kourtney Kardashian, but it was very close to that."

Then he humbly acknowledged some of the parallels between himself and Twain: "See, I always liked the way Mark Twain looked. Ya know, the shock of white hair, the handsome chiseled features.... Of course, if he looked like that today, he'd probably be replaced by a younger, more talented Jimmy Twain."

Eventually, he did give some authentic "thank-yous" at the end of his remarks—and paid a great compliment to the Mark Twain Prize itself. "This is kind of a cool award. Because there are so many of the awards in Hollywood where you kind of campaign for something, or your 'press agent' sees if you can get it. This is one of these things, you just get a call one day and they go 'Oh, you got this.' So, this means a tremendous amount to me, I am terribly touched by all this…thank you for the most wonderful night of my life."

CHAPTER TWENTY-FOUR

The Coup of Bill Murray

"I spent the weekend with Cappy, and was better off for it…
except physically."
—BILL MURRAY, 2016

Bill Murray is a tough man to reach. He doesn't have an agent; he doesn't have a scheduler; he doesn't have a booker. It's just him, his lawyer, and a 1-800 number that even film directors have to use to find him.

In 2016, when we wanted to give Bill Murray the Mark Twain Prize, the question wasn't *whether* to offer it to him, but *how* to offer it to him. Normally, we would reach out to a person's reps before sending a formal invite letter, but in this case, there were no reps to speak of, and we didn't have an address on file.

It seemed like we really only had one choice. The Kennedy Center wrote a letter to Bill Murray's lawyer, the only man we knew of who made regular contact with Bill. We never heard back.

We need to secure each honoree months in advance so that we can book talent, sell tickets, and prepare promotional materials. After our one semi-traditional path of communication was exhausted, some other folks at the Kennedy Center wanted to move on and pick someone else.

I pushed back and insisted we keep trying. Bill Mu
the funniest people in the world. He would be an hor
ties to Chicago in the last year of Obama's presidency. Anα ιυ ...,
his being difficult to contact was an argument in *favor* of honoring
him as soon as possible—the more challenging someone is to book,
the bigger an event it becomes if you can lock them down.

If we wanted to get to Bill Murray, I knew one other line of communication we could try. I have a buddy, Craig Johnson, who, in
addition to being the vice chairman of the investment banking firm
JMP Group and one of the owners of the Golden State Warriors, is an
avid golfer. It just so happened that Craig and Bill had become friends
when they played together at the Pebble Beach Pro Am.

I called Craig with the unorthodox request that he be our conduit
to offer Bill Murray the Mark Twain Prize. Craig, in turn, told me to
text him a "very short invite" to forward to Bill. I obliged with something like, "The Kennedy Center would like to offer you this year's
Mark Twain Prize." Sure enough, Bill Murray texted Craig back, with
the bare minimum: "Well, I guess so."

Soon, Bill asked for my information, and we exchanged texts and
emails, making me one of the very few people on the planet to have
Bill Murray's contact information.[10] Once we were connected, one of
the things we scheduled was Bill's visit to the White House.

On the day of the visit, I met up with Bill in the lobby at the
Four Seasons Hotel where he was staying. I was in a coat and tie;
Bill wasn't. He asked me if he needed to wear a tie when meeting the
president in the Oval Office, and I told him he was Bill Murray—he
was the one getting honored, so he could wear whatever he wanted.

"Well, could I wear my Cubs jacket?" he said.

---

10 It's me, Lorne Michaels, the Chicago Cubs, and Bill Murray's family; I don't
even think Dan Aykroyd made the cut.

We obviously can't predict what current events will be happening when we award the prize, but every once in a while, something happens that is *very* convenient. When we gave Bill Murray the Mark Twain Prize on October 23, 2016, it was just days before the Cubs went to the World Series for the first time since 1945. Of course we had to let Bill wear his Cubs jacket, even though the president was a White Sox fan.

In the Oval Office we took the obligatory photos of the president handing Bill the Mark Twain bust, and the president summed up the purpose of the prize and why Bill deserved to receive it. "This is the official Mark Twain Prize for American Humor that is given only to the funniest people in the world, who brought us joy and good cheer in our darkest moments. And I continue to believe that *Groundhog Day* is one of the funniest movies of all time."

Cappy McGarr, Bill Murray, and President Barack Obama share a laugh in the Oval Office as Murray admires the bust of Mark Twain.

Then they exchanged compliments (both of them said that the other's work had made a lot of people's lives better). Bill had agreed that while he was at the White House he would do a PSA to get people to sign up for the Affordable Care Act. There had been one condition—no script; he'd ad-lib.

So, they set up some cups for a makeshift game of putt-putt golf in the Oval Office and filmed what may have been the lowest-budget PSA of all time.

The premise of the video became a game of putt-putt in the Oval Office, at a dollar a hole. The staff initially put down some paper cups, but Bill insisted on glass because evidently, the "clink" of the ball hitting the cup was an essential comedic moment. They made some impromptu jabs at one another (including Obama reminding Bill that he doesn't normally let Cubs fans into the Oval Office), and then they got to the plug for healthcare.gov:

Murray: Ow! Ahh.

Obama: You all right?

Murray: Just my knee barks a little bit.

Obama: Yeah? Have you had it looked at?

Murray: Uhh, I don't…I don't have anyone to look at it. Just…it hurts.

Obama: What do you mean? You don't have health insurance?

Murray: Not really, no.

Obama: Well, look, Bill: you don't have to go without health insurance because these days, because of the Affordable Care Act, anybody can get health insurance and it doesn't matter if you already have something wrong with you because insur-

ance companies have to take you even if you have a preexist-
ing condition.

Murray: Are you saying mental health is covered too?

Obama: Mental health is covered as well.

Murray: Healthcare.gov…so you have to have a computer or
something like that. You go on a computer?

Obama: On your computer, you can go on your phone, you'll
be able to shop for the kind of insurance that's best for you.
(*Bill putts the ball into the glass.*)

Murray: Where does Michelle keep your money? Which
drawer is it in?

Obama: Just stay out of those drawers and don't press any of
those buttons. But remember to go to healthcare.gov.

Bill Murray and President Barack Obama take part in
a putt-putt contest in the Oval Office.

Bill buried all five balls he putted; the president missed every single one. Since the president had bet Bill a dollar a hole, he had to cough up five bucks. As the president doesn't carry any cash, he got one of his aides to hand Bill a fiver. I asked the president if I could take a picture of it, to which he said, "Of course not."

After a treat getting to putt with Bill on the Eisenhower Putting Green outside the Oval Office, we headed to the James S. Brady Press Briefing Room, where a briefing had just ended and there were only a few people left lingering around. I coaxed Bill into taking the press secretary's podium and said to him, "Mister President, do you think the Cubs will win?"

"I feel very confident that Clayton Kershaw is a great, great pitcher, but we've got too many sticks," he said, to laughter. "You get a little bit of autumn in Chicago," he went on, "you don't get that in Los Angeles. Trees just die in Los Angeles."

Finally, we took some stairs underneath the Press Room, where there used to be a swimming pool, but the Nixon administration had it covered up to accommodate a new press briefing room for the rise of TV news. Now, it's become a place where famous people (and their gawking associates) sign the plywood wall. Bill came upon a funny note that read, "I swam here.—Jimmy Kimmel."

Bill added, "...and I saved him.—Bill Murray."

And me? I left a clever note of my own: "CAPPY MCGARR."

✦ ✦ ✦

The rehearsal dinner honoring Bill Murray took place in the Supreme Court, which was (shockingly) the subject of a lot of controversy that year. President Obama had nominated Merrick Garland to replace the late Justice Antonin Scalia on the Supreme Court, but the Republicans were refusing to hold confirmation hearings until after that year's presidential election. I had to address the elephant in the room when I made my opening remarks.

"I have to confess," I said, "I'm a little embarrassed. For those of you who can't see, there are nine seats at the justice's table, but only eight guests. Mitch McConnell insisted we leave an empty chair."

And then I got to pay tribute to our honoree, and my White House touring buddy: "Tonight isn't about constitutional theory. Tonight is about comedy. We're here to honor the 2016 Mark Twain Prize winner, Bill Murray."

Applause.

"And tomorrow night, we'll gather at the Kennedy Center to honor the 2016 Mark Twain Prize winner, Bill Murray. Again."

Applause.

"What is this, *Groundhog Day*?"

The first toaster of the night was Jimmy Kimmel. He said "Pappy, thank you, that was a great introduction." After he finished, I came back to introduce the next comedian and clarified, "My name is Cappy, like a baseball cap."

Big mistake: I should have just let it go. After that, when I introduced Bill Hader, he started his toast with "Thank you, Slappy." It became the running gag of the evening to butcher my name in as many ways as possible—Nappy, Happy, Flappy, you name it, on and on and on.

At the following year's rehearsal dinner, Kimmel said that I didn't seem nervous emceeing, which is really a compliment to my acting ability. (Kimmel admitted being nervous anytime he performs, if you're wondering whether stage fright ever goes away.)

Anyway, after the snappy Cappy gag went on and on, the last toaster of the night, David Letterman, gave me some credit. He looked me in the eyes and said, "I don't know who you are, but you are doing a helluva good job." Honestly, I should print that on my business cards.

Bill Murray and Cappy McGarr pose with a topsy-turvy bust of Mark Twain.

The next day, the ceremony featured tributes from younger comedians who were inspired by Murray's work, like Aziz Ansari, Hader,
and Kimmel. Some of Murray's movie costars, like Emma Stone and
Sigourney Weaver, reflected on what it was like to work with him.
The stage was graced with dazzling musical performances from Paul

Shaffer, Miley Cyrus, and Rhiannon Giddens. And maybe the most meaningful tributes came from Bill's contemporaries and closest friends: Roy Blount Jr., Jane Curtin, and a freshly bearded post-retirement Letterman.

Kimmel, also freshly bearded, was our first speaker out of the gate and talked about the many urban legends that have accumulated about Bill Murray's interactions with the public. "There are hundreds of stories that, if they weren't about Bill Murray, you'd read them in the biography *The World's Most Arrested Man*."

Later, after a montage of the best moments from Bill Murray's "Nick the Lounge Singer" character, Paul Shaffer accompanied Miley Cyrus as she sang perhaps the most intensely hard-rock rendition of Frank Sinatra's "My Way" ever performed. (There was twerking and strobe lights.)

The final speaker to give a tribute that night was maybe the most elusive figure of the evening besides Bill Murray himself: David Letterman. He had quit his show in 2015, and the most that anyone had seen from Dave around that time was a few scattered paparazzi photos of him with scraggly facial hair in the mountains of Montana. But Dave—in his typically self-deprecating fashion—made clear just how highly he thought of Bill Murray: "I have two observations. One: I wonder if the collective talent of the people we have been treated to performing here tonight on this stage are truly equal to the talent of this man sitting in the box right up there. My other observation is, Jimmy Kimmel, the beard is not working."

At the end of his remarks, Dave introduced a montage of Bill Murray's wildest entrances to Dave's set over the years. It included everything from a fully choreographed performance of "Let's Get Physical" to flying into the studio as Peter Pan.

And then it was Murray's turn to speak. The first thing he did once he got on stage was that he took the Mark Twain bust, and—in a hilarious move that nonetheless gave the executive producers a heart attack—handed it to the audience for them to pass around to the back so everyone could touch it.

He then gave an uncharacteristically sentimental speech: crediting his brother, Brian Doyle-Murray, who was in attendance, for much of his own success, paying tribute to the promise of America, and expressing gratitude for the privilege of living a prosperous, happy life.

He also made sure to comment on the Cubs having won Game 6 the night before, securing their place in the World Series: "I'm glad that they won last night so I could be here this evening. If they hadn't won last night, I would have had to have been there, because honestly, I do not trust the media to report the score accurately."

After some brief "thank-yous," and singing a rousing rendition of the old blues standard "Sweet Home Chicago," Bill exited the stage.

A couple of weeks later, the Chicago Cubs won the World Series for the first time in 108 years. Between that and the Mark Twain Prize, it was an incredible couple of weeks, witnessing both Bill Murray and his beloved baseball team achieve respective victories that were long overdue.

Afterward, I got a lovely email from Bill with his reflections on the whole experience.

Hey, Cappy,

What a day and what wonderful photos! It looks as good as I remember it. Gonna miss this guy, aren't we. Thanks one million times for taking me around the House, meeting all the people working inside made an indelible impression on me. And putting over the Affordable Health Care Act...geez, I felt like George M. Cohan in there, as good a citizen as I could be, a booster shot for the democracy to come

It was the most American experience of my life, and I have you to thank for it. The tour for my family! All you can eat dinner at the Supreme Court! Where you were very funny, sir. Honestly, it hasn't sunk in yet. I will write letters, I swear. Right after Pebble Beach. Please take care of yourself, friend,

Bill

Bill Murray was so cordial and humble throughout his visit. When we were being escorted by White House staffers, he made a point of chatting with everyone. When we dropped by the White House kitchen, he stopped and talked to all the people working there. It didn't matter who you were or what your job was; he was the same down-to-earth, funny guy with everybody.

Bill has a reputation of randomly appearing at the most unusual places and times, but what the public might not realize is that once he pops up somewhere, he's a complete gentleman. And the Mark Twain Prize would not be the last time I observed that to be true.

✦ ✦ ✦

By 2018, Janie and I had accumulated in our home nearly two decades' worth of massive autographed posters commemorating the Mark Twain Prize ceremonies, and we decided that it was time to donate them; we chose UT Austin's Harry Ransom Center. The dean of the communication school, Jay Bernhardt, and I wanted to host a quick event to commemorate the donation, and we wanted some star power to up the ante.

There was only one man for the job. I reached out to Bill Murray; after a few quick emails, he was in. It was easier to book him for this ceremony than it was for the Mark Twain Prize.

In the press conference I played up the faux-significance of the event:

"It is my pleasure to be here today at UT's Belo Center for New Media," I said, "for what I believe is one of the greatest moments in American culture. Now all of you know the University of Texas Harry

Ransom Center is home to some of history's most significant artifacts. There are just five copies of the Gutenberg Bible in the United States. One of them is there. The first photograph was taken nearly two centuries ago. Where is it kept safe? You guessed it: the Ransom Center. Even with these prized possessions—these cultural benchmarks—it always felt like something was missing. It felt like the Ransom Center had yet to capture the magnitude of human artistic achievement."

Then I wiped a (sarcastic) tear, before continuing:

"Well, I'm here to change all that today. It's my honor to donate what can only be described as history's greatest cultural artifacts: the complete collection of the commemorative posters from the Kennedy Center Mark Twain Prize for American Humor. And unlike that sorry first photograph, these posters are in color."

Finally, I introduced Bill Murray, who got straight to the biggest question on everyone's minds: "Perhaps you could tell me why *you're* here. Because I have no idea why *I'm* here."

Bill then spent most of his remarks wondering aloud just how exactly I had come into his life: "Cappy just keeps buggin' ya and you end up doing things. You don't know why. I still don't know what he does. I heard that extensive biography; we still can't figure out what he does, except he's kind of an autograph collector, I guess. I don't know what he does for a living. I have no idea. I think he's the spook, I think he's CIA or something, but I don't know."[11]

And then came my favorite dig: "I see that there's a video camera here. Now I'm going to have to testify about what I knew about Cappy and when."

Eventually, Bill did say some very kind things about my work as executive producer of the Mark Twain Prize, and my performance at the rehearsal dinner: "Cappy really did make [the ceremony] go. And I was very impressed with how funny he was in the Supreme Court.

---

11 This was a rejected blurb for this book.

He actually got a lot of laughs in this sacred temple of America which is a beautiful place. I had no idea he was actually gonna be funny."

It's a somewhat backhanded compliment I've gotten again and again, but I will always be grateful when *anybody* describes me as "surprisingly funny," let alone Bill Murray. Bill closed out his remarks with one last invitation to interrogate my identity: "Does anybody have any questions they'd like to ask me…about Cappy?"

I have one: How did I get so lucky to end up the subject of an impromptu roast from Bill Murray?

At the Cappy's Place coffee shop at UT Austin, Bill Murray salutes Xavier University, where his son Luke was an assistant basketball coach. Also pictured: Cappy McGarr and Dean Jay Bernhardt.

Left: A caricature of Cappy McGarr by Robert Risko welcomes visitors to Cappy's Place, a coffee shop at UT's Belo Center for New Media.

CHAPTER TWENTY-FIVE

The King of Late Night and the Queen of Sitcoms

Our next two honorees represented the pinnacle of their respective television comedy worlds. In 2017, we paid tribute to a late-night legend who spent over three decades on the air, and in 2018, a sitcom star who had been consistently adored by critics and audiences alike. The twentieth and twenty-first recipients of the Mark Twain Prize were David Letterman and Julia Louis-Dreyfus.

Giving David Letterman the Mark Twain Prize was a total no-brainer, and the Bill Murray ceremony the year before had proven that Dave would emerge for an event at the Kennedy Center. Even so, Dave's acceptance still marked a rare public appearance from the retired king of late night. Or, at least, retired from network: in the time between our announcement that Dave would be the twentieth recipient of the Mark Twain Prize and the ceremony itself, Netflix announced that it would be debuting a new long-form interview show with Letterman hosting.

When I emceed the rehearsal dinner celebrating David Letterman at the Renwick Gallery, the first thing I had to address was Dave's newly-developed unshaven "Mountain Man" appearance. I took the podium donning a big fake scraggly white beard at the beginning of my remarks and asked Dave, "How do you wear this thing all day? It's so itchy."

That was followed by some jokes about the shaky state of American politics. (This was the first Mark Twain Prize since Donald Trump became the occupant of the White House.)

Dave had met Trump—in fact, Trump had been a perennial guest more than thirty times on *Late Night* and *The Late Show* over the years, before announcing his run for president. But Dave had no interest in visiting Trump in the Oval Office. Later, when he was asked about his relationship with Trump, Dave diplomatically responded, "He used to be kind of like the boob of New York that pretended to be wealthy, or we thought was wealthy, and now he's just a psychotic."

Anyway, I stayed the hell away from saying the president's name, but I managed to get a sly joke in on him nonetheless: "Last year's Twain honoree was Bill Murray. We all loved the movie *Caddyshack*, where he played a character who ranted incoherently and spent all his time on the golf course. Sound like anyone we know?"

Eventually, I got around to praising the comedy royalty in the room: "Over his thirty-three-year, Emmy Award-winning late-night run, David has been one-of-a-kind; somehow managing to be surprisingly inane, surprisingly profound, and always funny. As the longest-serving late-night host in television history, he is the best argument against term limits. He is a television legend and an inspiration to an entire generation of comedians."

The next day at the ceremony, we had folks from Dave's era of comedy—Jimmie Walker, Martin Short, and previous Mark Twain Prize recipients Steve Martin and Bill Murray—and comedians from the generation inspired by him, like Jimmy Kimmel, Norm MacDonald, and Amy Schumer. Senator Al Franken (D-MN) made a rare comedic appearance, Pearl Jam's Eddie Vedder performed music, and there was a set from John Mulaney, who described himself as the obligatory "stand-up comedian that no one in the audience recognized."

A scraggly David Letterman shakes hands with a clean-shaven Cappy McGarr.

But what made that year's ceremony unique was the way we paid tribute to Dave and his legendary television program. Every year, the Mark Twain Prize ceremony features a boisterous announcer and a killer house band. But it was only this year that we booked *The Late Show* announcer Alan Kalter, along with Paul Shaffer and the World's Most Dangerous Band. With them, the talent paying tribute, and a guest appearance by Letterman's former stage manager Biff Henderson, the evening played out like one final blow-out bonus episode of *The Late Show with David Letterman*. In fact, Biff delivered one of the best gags of the night. He walked on while a strange noise played in the background, and he identified it as "Mark Twain rolling in his grave."

The show began with one of the most theatrical entrances the Mark Twain Prize has ever seen: Steve Martin and Martin Short were rolled onto the stage—with Steve Martin at the piano and Martin Short *on* the piano.

Short: We are so excited to be here for the Mark Twain Prize, celebrating a man we all know and tolerate: David Letterman.

Martin: You know, Marty, when the show started, I didn't really realize it was a celebration for David Letterman... because of the applause.

Short: And on a sober note—because they didn't send champagne—it says a lot about America when people of different white backgrounds can gather together like this.

Later that night, Eddie Vedder performed an emotional rendition of Warren Zevon's "Keep Me in Your Heart," accompanied by Paul Shaffer and the World's Most Dangerous Band and a six-piece backing vocal group. Zevon had appeared on Letterman's show many times throughout the eighties and nineties, sometimes filling in as bandleader when Paul Shaffer was away. In 2002, after Zevon was diagnosed with lung cancer, he appeared on Dave's show one last time. He was the only guest for the entire hour. The two men candidly discussed Zevon's diagnosis, his life, and his career. Zevon passed away the next year, after which Dave and Paul paid tribute to the man and his legacy. Nearly fifteen years later, that legacy was on full display for the audience in the Kennedy Center and across the country, in the midst of a night encapsulating Dave's life and career.

Just before David Letterman was introduced, much of the talent from that evening came out to deliver a final Letterman-sanctioned "Top 10 List." The category was "Top 10 Differences Between Mark Twain and David Letterman."

10. Jimmy Kimmel: "Dave's name isn't Mark."
9. Steve Martin: "Twain never lied to me about being a fan of the banjo."
8. Jimmie Walker: "Twain never finished a show and sat in a dark office weeping for 3 hours."

7. Chris Elliott: "I'm sorry, Dave, I was sound asleep backstage. What are you doing out here, like a little Top 10 kinda thing? What is that, like a lot of jokes, something like that? Yeah, I don't do jokes. But I'll give you a little soft shoe." *(Chris then danced a soft shoe, with Paul Shaffer's accompaniment.)*

6. Amy Schumer: "Mark Twain was Sam Clemens's riverboat name. Dave's nautical pen name is Rear Admiral."

5. Norm MacDonald: "Mark Twain was considered a highly entertaining public speaker."

4. John Mulaney: "Twain would have mastered the simple process of text messaging."

3. Bill Murray: "Only one wrote his best material on coke binges with Louisa May Alcott."

2. Martin Short: "Two words: 'Netflix Sellout.'"

1. Paul Shaffer: "I've actually been invited to Mark Twain's house."

Finally, we were treated to a hilarious monologue from a man who had delivered thousands over the course of his career. David Letterman took the stage and asked the question no one was thinking: "Is it wrong that I kind of wish this could have been presented posthumously?"

Dave then "borrowed" a copy of that night's commemorative poster from the band and, one-by-one, praised the talent who had paid tribute to him. Just one year earlier, at the previous Mark Twain Prize ceremony, he had wondered aloud whether Bill Murray had more talent than all of the other comedians paying tribute combined. Now, Dave was demurring and asserting that he wasn't worthy of all the praise he had just been given.

His thoughts on Martin Short? "Why has this person not received this award?" On Amy Schumer? "Future recipient of this award." On Bill Murray? "Should have received a car with his award."

Then, ever the humble Indianan, Dave continued: "Here I am tonight receiving this award, and I ask myself: How did this happen? And I'll tell you how it happened. It wasn't because of me. It was because of hundreds and hundreds and hundreds, perhaps thousands, of people who helped me. And you saw some of my friends here tonight, all of them more talented, more gifted, funnier than I am. But they all helped me. And I would just like to say: we have to help each other, or nothing will happen."

Dave closed with a quote from Mark Twain that felt especially appropriate, given the political moment: "There's a million quotes from Mark Twain, and I'm gonna wrap this up now with [one], and I hope I get it correct . . . . Mark Twain's definition of patriotism is this: 'Patriotism is supporting your country all the time, and your government when it deserves it.'"

✦ ✦ ✦

A quick aside about working with Eddie Vedder on this show: When I helped put together the Gershwin Prize honoring Paul McCartney—which I'll share more about later—I met a guy in the Secret Service at the White House named Mike Lotus, and we ended up becoming good friends.

In the run-up to the Letterman ceremony, Mike, who was friends with Eddie, invited us (along with Eddie's wife, Jill, and their manager) on a tour he was taking of the US Capitol. This wasn't just any tour; renovations had just been completed, and we were going to tour all the way up the cast iron dome to the *tholos*.

If you're like me, you had to google what a *tholos* is. Turns out, it's the *pointy top part beneath the Statue of Freedom*. Whatever you call it, it offered a spectacular panoramic view of DC.

On the tour, we climbed long winding stairs until we reached the *tholos*—a word which I'll bring up in conversation as much as I can, having looked it up. A Capitol security guard came up with us, making sure we got up there safely. For some time, we quietly appreciated the scenery. Eventually, the security guard approached me and asked, "May I say something to Eddie?"

I told him he didn't need to ask my permission. I let Eddie know the security guard had something to say. Eddie thanked the guard for the tour, and the guard said: "Mister Vedder, I've been to over thirty-five of your concerts. I went through a tough time and—"

Tears welled from the security guard's eyes. He was a big, stoic guy; this came out of the blue. "Thanks for getting me through tough times," he said. "I wouldn't have made it without you."

Now, since the rest of us weren't made of stone, we started wiping tears too. Eddie responded, "From now on, you've got a backstage pass. Come to any concert of mine you want."

It was like something out of a heartwarming reality show, except it wasn't staged and inspiring music was only playing in my head. That moment redoubled my faith in show business folks. At their best, even their small gestures change people's lives for the better. Whether you're David Letterman or a Capitol security guard—given the chance, Eddie Vedder will brighten your day.

Cappy McGarr and Eddie Vedder pose atop the Capitol tholos.

Left: Jill Vedder, Eddie Vedder, Cappy McGarr, and Eddie Vedder's team pose in the Capitol rotunda.

✦ ✦ ✦

In 2018, we gave the Mark Twain Prize to Julia Louis-Dreyfus. I could go on and on about how wonderful and talented she is, except that I already did that when I emceed her rehearsal dinner at the Folger Shakespeare Library: "In the entertainment business," I said, "if you can manage to be a part of one hit TV show, you're lucky. If you can manage to be a part of two hit shows, you're an anomaly. Three, you're a legend. And four [*Saturday Night Live, Seinfeld, The New Adventures of Old Christine*, and *Veep*]...well, you're Julia Louis-Dreyfus.

"In doing all of this, she has debunked all notions of a *Seinfeld* curse. The only '*Seinfeld* curse' she has to endure is the onslaught of residual checks that will follow her for the rest of her life. We don't begrudge her this, though. America loves a 'riches to even greater riches' story."

Then, I felt the need to get serious, even if just for a moment. About one year prior, Julia had announced that she had been diagnosed with breast cancer. I had the privilege of letting her know how much her fight meant to me. "Julia, if I can be personal for a moment, my mother's a breast cancer survivor. I have to tell you, you have inspired all of us with the way you handled your own diagnosis and battle. You shared…inspired…and persevered. Thank you."

She looked me in the eyes and mouthed "thank you" right back.

There was just one line that I decided to cut from my rehearsal dinner remarks. After a lengthy confirmation battle, Brett Kavanaugh had just ascended to the Supreme Court. And it just so happened that he and Julia Louis-Dreyfus had grown up in the same town, a town that Kavanaugh had said familiarized him with the scourge of gun violence…which would have made sense if he was actually from DC, but he was from the tony suburb of Bethesda, Maryland.

So, I was *going* to say: "In some ways, it's a miracle that Julia made it this far, growing up walking the mean streets of Bethesda, Maryland, a community that, as we all recently learned from our newest Supreme Court justice, is just riddled with gun violence. Some places have Crips and Bloods. Bethesda had lacrosse and Bretts."

Ultimately, I didn't think it would be appropriate. As a Kennedy Center board member, there are certain lines I just can't cross. Sure, it's okay for Brett Kavanaugh to sit on the Supreme Court, but God forbid I make a joke about him.

Julia and I had met before; we had both been invited by President Obama to a state dinner honoring the president of France. That night, I had the chance to meet Julia's father, who had since passed away. I told her all of this, not expecting her to remember, but she said, "We met in the China Room!" I told her the cut Kavanaugh joke too—she laughed and said: "That's really good. Don't worry about it. In my acceptance remarks, I'm going to go over that *plenty*."

✦ ✦ ✦

At Julia's ceremony, the talent included Jerry Seinfeld, Bryan Cranston, and a video from Larry David. From Chicago's legendary Second City theater group where Julia came up, we had Tina Fey, Stephen Colbert, and Keegan-Michael Key. We also had Julia's longtime friend and fellow sitcom star Lisa Kudrow, her hilarious *Veep* co-star Tony Hale, and up-and-coming comedians like Kumail Nanjiani, Ilana Glazer, and Abbi Jacobson.

Stephen Colbert gave the opening monologue, and shared a delightfully self-aware compliment: "What a joy it is tonight to honor the great Julia Louis-Dreyfus, a woman who I sincerely believe is the funniest person on television. And keep in mind, I'm on television right now."

Tina Fey revealed her theory about how Julia had become so successful: "Here's the secret: Julia's not afraid to be unlikable. Not on screen, and not in person."

Keegan-Michael Key—much like Alec Baldwin before him at Tina Fey's ceremony—came out as Mark Twain with the signature white suit, ridiculously exaggerated mustache, and scrappy wig. He said: "Welcome, everybody, to the Me Prize for American Humor. When I was growing up a small white boy in Hannibal, Missouri, I never thought that one day I'd find myself handing out a likeness of my own head to trailblazers of tomfoolery, bastions of buffoonery, and in this particular case, a heroine of herculean humor!"

Ilana Glazer and Abbi Jacobson of *Broad City* fame paid tribute in a more abstract, interpretive fashion—by leading over half a dozen dancers in a blown-out choreographed version of the "Elaine Dance" from *Seinfeld*.

Finally, at the end of the night, a visibly emotional Julia Louis-Dreyfus took the stage to accept the Mark Twain Prize:

"When Mark Twain first emailed me about the Mark Twain Prize, I have to admit I totally misunderstood. I assumed that I was being asked to honor somebody else who was receiving the Mark Twain Prize, and I thought, 'Oh my God, what a hassle.' I mean seriously, who would put me through this? I have to go all the way to Washington, DC, which, no offense, is a nightmare, and make up flattering things to say about how funny someone *else* is? No f**king way. And then I reread the email. And I realized, 'Oh, it's me! They're giving it to me! I get the prize!' And my attitude about the whole thing changed, it really did."

And, as promised, she laid into Kavanaugh: "Back in fourth grade, as a matter of fact, I was in a very serious Holton-Arms production of *Serendipity*. You know it's funny with us Holton girls. I remember every detail of that play. I could swear to it under penalty of perjury. And yet, I don't remember who drove me to the show or who drove me home. Or if Squee or Tobin were there. Or if Brett put it on his weird wall calendar."

Later, in a beautifully vulnerable moment, Julia's voice cracked as she addressed her recent cancer diagnosis and the essential role that laughter played in her recovery: "Laughter is a basic human need, along with love and food and an HBO subscription. There's no situation—none—that isn't improved with a couple of laughs. Everybody needs laughs. So the fact that I've had the opportunity to make people laugh for a living is one of the many blessings that I have received in my life."

That's why we give out this award. You can't beat that.

CHAPTER TWENTY-SIX

Chappelle's Prize

Sometimes, we give the Mark Twain Prize to a comedian who has left a lasting legacy for the entertainers who have followed in their footsteps. Other times, we give the Mark Twain Prize to someone whose best work may yet be ahead of them. Sometimes, we give the Prize to a veteran stand-up comedian with hours upon hours of material. Other times, we give the Prize to a television mogul who revolutionized the medium of sketch comedy. We've given it to brilliant writers; we've given it to versatile actors; we've given it to extraordinary producers.

Do you see what I'm getting at? On October 27, 2019, we gave the twenty-second Mark Twain Prize for American Humor to Dave Chappelle, who somehow fits *all* of these criteria.

For *Chappelle's Show* alone, Dave would have qualified. But since then, he's put out numerous Netflix specials, won Emmys and Grammys, and received the two honors every comedian strives for: critical acclaim and social media outrage.

The night before the show, I emceed the rehearsal dinner at the National Museum of African American History and Culture, and I got to pay tribute to Dave:

"It's so incredible to be here at the National Museum of African American History and Culture," I said. "As I look around this room, I can't think of anyone better to celebrate the achievements of a groundbreaking African American comedian than the likes of Morgan Freeman, Tiffany Haddish…and me? Are you kidding me? Okay, we'll see how this goes!"

I continued in that vein: "On *Chappelle's Show*, Dave created such memorable characters as Silky Johnson, Clayton Bigsby, and Tyrone Biggums—none of whom have a single quote I am allowed to repeat."

At every one of these rehearsal dinners, I have to strike the balance of delivering funny material without getting myself in trouble. And I probably toed that line the most when I was introducing our first toaster of the night, Tiffany Haddish: "Last year was a big year for Tiffany. She won her first Emmy award, she's been on the cover of *Time* magazine, and she hosted an episode of the show *Drunk History*. For those of you who don't know, *Drunk History* is where a celebrity drinks a bunch of alcohol, then tells a long, rambling, pseudo-intellectual story. So she's well-prepared for a night at the Kennedy Center."

Then I had a follow-up: "Don't worry though, unlike *Drunk History*, no one is going to see this weekend's festivities…not because they won't be on TV, but because they'll be on PBS."

Finally, when Tiffany Haddish took the stage, I gave her a kiss on the cheek, and she proudly announced: "That's the first time this year I've been kissed by a white man!"

As she opened up her toast, she erroneously referred to me as Lorne Michaels and Kennedy Center chairman David Rubenstein as Steve Martin. (Because, y'know, all white-haired guys look alike.)

Then, Tiffany caught me laughing hard at one of her jokes and called me out: "He's turnin' red. That's what I love about white men. Your heart beatin' fast…I don't want your wife gettin' mad at me for giving you mouth-to-mouth!"

Finally, I got about as political as I could get when introducing Morgan Freeman: "Morgan has played everyone from the president of the United States to a common criminal. There was a time when that took range."

Cappy McGarr and Morgan Freeman share a private moment in front of large audience at the National Museum of African American History and Culture.

The next day happened to be Sunday, October 27, the same night that the Nats were playing Game 5 of the World Series *in Washington*. Despite the conflict in programming, the ceremony was jam-packed: it featured comedians Chappelle came up with and has collaborated with over the years, like Sarah Silverman, Aziz Ansari, and Jon Stewart. Also in appearance were Tiffany Haddish, Trevor Noah, Kenan Thompson, Michael Che, and Colin Jost; some of Dave's celebrity buddies showed up too, like Bradley Cooper, Yasiin Bey, Q-Tip, Common, Erykah Badu, Frédéric Yonnet, and John Legend. And then there was the comedy godfather himself, former Twain Prize winner Lorne Michaels.

Sarah Silverman was dumbfounded: "Dave, can you believe this? You're getting the freaking Mark Twain Prize? It's actually perfect that you're getting the Mark Twain Prize because you both love using the n-word in your masterpieces."

But it was Jon Stewart who cut to the core of what makes Dave so special. He rightly referred to *Chappelle's Show* as what it is: a "cultural phenomenon." And he reflected on the time that Comedy Central was bending over backwards to get Dave to go through with a third season, even as he felt that the show was becoming something he couldn't stand by: "They offered Dave fifty million dollars to just give us one more.... But Dave, at that moment, was conflicted because of how difficult the show was to do, because he wondered about its impact on the audience that he meant it for. And he wondered if the creative process wasn't right for it. And he walked away...and it was that moment that I remember thinking, 'Comedy Central has fifty million dollars?'"

And then it was Dave's turn, and he did The Mark Twain Prize his way. He got up on stage, lit a cigarette ("What are they gonna do? Kick me out before I get the prize?"), and talked about how comedy saved his life.

Having been no stranger to controversy throughout his career—and admitting that he didn't write a speech in advance—Dave spoke freely and honestly about the direction he felt comedy was going, defending the right of comedians to say whatever they want, however they want, in pursuit of getting a laugh and telling the truth (in that order):

"Man, it's not that serious. The First Amendment is first for a reason. The Second is just in case the first one doesn't work out."

Dave Chappelle and Cappy McGarr at Chappelle's Mark Twain Prize rehearsal dinner at the National Museum of African American History and Culture.

CHAPTER TWENTY-SEVEN

The Gershwin Prize

In addition to the Mark Twain Prize, I've had the chance to produce a few shows at Washington's other most esteemed comedy venue: the White House. One set of those shows was an annual honor created in 2007: the Library of Congress Gershwin Prize for Popular Song.

The team behind the Gershwin Prize included Peter Kaminsky, Bob Kaminsky, Mark Krantz, and me: all creators of the Mark Twain Prize. In addition, Dalton Delan, the chief programming officer of the PBS station WETA in Washington, DC, had executive-produced the Mark Twain Prize ceremony since it moved to PBS in 2000, and he would also be a key creator of the Gershwin Prize.

Peter had gone to Princeton University, where he took classes from and became close with his history professor, James H. Billington. As decades passed, they maintained a great relationship, which endured as Jim Billington became the nation's thirteenth Librarian of Congress in 1987. And the Library of Congress has an extensive archive of recordings and manuscripts from many of the best American musicians, making it a natural fit to sponsor a prize honoring songwriters.

But first, we needed a namesake. For a while, we considered calling it the Stephen Foster Prize. But we realized that not that many people would know about his career without googling. We wanted a name that would make honorees say, "Wow, what an honor!" and not "Who?"

Around that time, Peter and his wife, Melinda, had my family and me over for a barbecue at his house in Brooklyn. As we chatted, we agreed that we needed a more legendary namesake. Then, my daughter Kathryn made a suggestion: "What about George Gershwin?" Peter immediately took to it, and he suggested that it be named after both brothers in the duo: George and Ira Gershwin. To honor them both, it would simply be called the "Gershwin Prize."

It was the perfect fit for what we were trying to accomplish. Together, George and Ira Gershwin had written some of the most unforgettable songs and musicals of the twentieth century. Their songs included "Embraceable You," "Let's Call the Whole Thing Off," and "I Got Rhythm," along with musicals like *Of Thee I Sing*, *Let 'Em Eat Cake*, and *Lady, Be Good*.

Additionally, naming the prize after the Gershwins would be a great fit for the Library of Congress, considering that the Library had an extensive collection of the Gershwins' materials, including their sketchbooks, music manuscripts, photographs, legal documents, and even Ira's typewriter and George's piano. And, perhaps most importantly, like "Twain," the name "Gershwin" immediately invokes gravitas: the name of two all-time great songwriters.

With the name decided, Peter went to the Library of Congress, met with Jim Billington, the Librarian of Congress, and pitched the idea. Jim took to it immediately, and the Library of Congress went to the families of George and Ira Gershwin to get approval for the use of the Gershwin name. They agreed, which is unusual for both sides of the Gershwin family, and we could begin to prepare the first show. For context, when we would arrange seating for the Gershwin Prize ceremonies, I was responsible for keeping the Gershwin families happy and separate. (What made them happy was being separate.)

The executive producers of the show got together to decide who the inaugural recipient of the Gershwin Prize would be, and it didn't take long for us to come to consensus: we chose the great Paul Simon. He was the perfect musician to receive the honor: between his collaborations with Art Garfunkel and his solo work, Paul Simon had won twelve Grammy Awards, he had been inducted into the Rock & Roll Hall of Fame *twice* (as a solo musician and as one-half of Simon & Garfunkel), and his music is simply iconic, with albums like *Bridge Over Troubled Water*, *Still Crazy After All These Years*, and *Graceland* all being classics.

We held the first Gershwin Prize ceremony on May 23, 2007, at the Warner Theater in Washington, DC, and the lineup of star performers who agreed to come and celebrate Paul Simon was wonderful—Lyle Lovett, Buckwheat Zydeco, Yolanda Adams, Jerry Douglas, Stephen Marley, Shawn Colvin, Ladysmith Black Mambazo, The Dixie Hummingbirds, James Taylor, Alison Krauss, Philip Glass, Stevie Wonder, and Marc Anthony, who was perhaps the best performer that night.

And, in something of a coup, Art Garfunkel agreed to perform with Paul Simon on the show; they had done one reunion tour a couple of years earlier, and the occasional one-off performance here and there, but you never knew whether their relationship would be on-again or off-again—for the Gershwin Prize, it was on-again.

At the ceremony, Paul took the stage and sang "Diamonds on the Soles of Her Shoes," from *Graceland*, before introducing his longtime "dear friend, and partner in arguments" Art Garfunkel, for a performance of "Bridge Over Troubled Water." Paul followed that up with "Father and Daughter" and then brought up Stevie Wonder to join him on "Me and Julio Down by the Schoolyard" and "Loves Me like a Rock." Finally, the night concluded with Philip Glass performing a somber rendition of "The Sound of Silence."

Paul was humble and gracious in his acceptance speech, saying, "I'm amazed to find myself in this great room, receiving this award that puts my work in the context of the genius of the Gershwins. It's simply impossible for me to comprehend that the music I wrote—which came from my generation, from the heart, from my parents—could have affected people over the course of the years and in such a way."

Paul was totally hands-on for the whole process; he showed up for every rehearsal and worked with all the musicians. A moment that continues to stick out in my mind came when Lyle Lovett was rehearsing "50 Ways to Leave Your Lover." As Lovett was running through it, Paul approached him and said, "You don't have the cadence right, and your timing is a little off. Do it one more time." Lyle tried again, and before he could finish Paul cut him off, and asked, "Do you mind if I sing in your ear so you can hear what it should sound like?" He did, Lyle got it right, Paul said, "That's perfect," and they moved on.

I was horrified. Was this going to make Lyle upset? I had worked with him before, from back when he played our kickoff DASHPAC fundraiser; I was the one to reach out to him for this show, and I felt responsible for making sure he was comfortable. After rehearsal, I grabbed a burger with him, and I told him I was sorry if he was embarrassed by Paul correcting him. Lyle just laughed. "Cappy, do you realize how cool it is to have Paul Simon singing '50 Ways to Leave Your Lover' in your ear? Are you kidding me? I loved it!"

Paul was a joy to work with, and between his fantastic performance and all the wonderful people who came to pay him tribute, it made for a perfect inaugural Gershwin Prize. And its success, of course, helped us ensure it wouldn't be the *only* Gershwin Prize.

✦　✦　✦

The next year, the Library of Congress announced that Stevie Wonder would be the second recipient of the Gershwin Prize. That year, with Dalton Delan's help, we partnered with the PBS affiliate station WETA, which had a long-running recurring series called *In Performance at the White House*, to host the ceremony in the East Room of the White House, with the president presenting the award for the very first time.

The selection of Stevie Wonder was announced in late 2008, but the ceremony wasn't held until February 2009, just weeks after the inauguration of President Barack Obama. Here was the first Black president, one month into his term, presenting an award to one of the country's most beloved Black artists of all time, during Black History Month. Obama had used the song "Signed, Sealed, Delivered (I'm Yours)" at just about every rally since he started his 2008 run for the presidency, and unlike a lot of artists whose songs are played by politicians (often against their will), Stevie approved, and even sang it at the 2008 Democratic National Convention.

I had had a wonderful experience meeting Stevie Wonder once before, years earlier, when he was receiving the Kennedy Center Honors in 1999. My daughter Elizabeth was a superfan of his, and as the secretary of state's pre-show dinner for the honorees was coming up, I asked George Stevens Jr., the creator of the Kennedy Center Honors, if there was any way she could be seated at Stevie Wonder's table. George made it happen, and Elizabeth had one of the most special nights of her life.

I approached Stevie that night in 1999, and I thanked him for being so friendly to Elizabeth. Then Stevie gave me a big hug, and he started tapping my shoulder with his fingers. I asked him what he was doing, and he said, "I'm playing a song for you."

It was a small moment, but it meant so much to me. Fast forward to 2009, and there were plenty of artists who were delighted to perform on a night in his honor. The show had tribute performances from Anita Johnson, India.Arie, Esperanza Spalding, Wayne Brady, Diana Krall, Martina McBride, Mary Mary, will.i.am, and Tony

Bennett, as well as a repeat performance from Paul Simon honoring Stevie, just as Stevie had honored him in 2007.

Michelle Obama introduced Stevie Wonder and shared that she "fell in love" with his music when she was a kid and that Stevie's song "You and I" was her and Barack's wedding song—underscoring how significant it was that they got to host him at the White House for this tribute.

After the intro, Stevie played classic songs like "Sir Duke," "Superstition," "Isn't She Lovely" (dedicated to Michelle and the first daughters), and, of course, "Signed, Sealed, Delivered (I'm Yours)." He brought down the house. It was—at least up to that point, I can confidently say—the funkiest moment in White House history. We had limited time with the president and the first lady in the East Room of the White House, but that didn't stop Stevie from stopping and starting "Signed, Sealed, Delivered (I'm Yours)" over again three or four times after messing up the intro.

President Obama gave a great speech, summarizing the massive impact Stevie had on his life, and on the world: "I think it's fair to say that had I not been a Stevie Wonder fan, Michelle might not have dated me. We might not have married. So, the fact that we agreed on Stevie was part of the essence of our courtship. And I'm not alone. Millions of people around the world have found similar comfort and joy in Stevie's music and his unique capacity to find hope in struggle, and humanity in our common hardships."

It was an amazing show that solidified the White House as the perfect venue for the Gershwin Prize. That location made the award feel like that much more of an honor to receive—not to mention the convenience for the president, whose commute to the ceremony would continue to be nonexistent.

✦　✦　✦

In 2010, we honored Sir Paul McCartney. This is where I would explain why he was selected and where I would attempt to summarize his career, but come on. He's Paul McCartney—you know, of the Beatles, and Wings, and, well, himself. He may not have been born in the United States, but his music has had a greater impact on the American zeitgeist than just about anyone; so in my mind, just as with Lorne Michaels and the Mark Twain Prize, there's no disputing his qualification for the honor.

We had a closed-off rehearsal the day before the show that consisted exclusively of Paul, his band, and the executive producers, in order to minimize distractions. Or, from my perspective, Paul McCartney treated me and the other executive producers to a private concert.

And there was no moment more otherworldly than when Paul rehearsed the final song, "Hey Jude." He got partway through the song when he stopped and asked where his guests and the first family would be sitting. Then he had Bob Kaminsky and me sit in the audience in those spots—one chair apart from each other—and he sang "Hey Jude" right between us. It felt like a dream.

We managed to deal with only one major show-threatening snafu. Paul wanted to bring his bodyguard to the White House for the show. His bodyguard carried a weapon and followed Paul everywhere he went. You can't blame Paul for wanting him there, given that he's one of the most famous people in the world, and especially considering what happened to John Lennon. But the Secret Service had nixed the bodyguard's guest credentials because, well, the Secret Service is at the White House, making it one of the safest places on earth.

Unbeknownst to me, another producer put the bodyguard's name back on the list—as a member of the production, not labeled as a bodyguard. But the Secret Service isn't stupid. In fact, not being stupid is kind of their job description. They caught it, and they were unwavering, telling us under no circumstances could Paul's body-guard come to the White House.

The show was supposed to start at 7:00 p.m. At four, I got a pan-icked call from Paul's manager, Barrie Marshall, who said, "Paul's not coming to the White House to do the show unless his bodyguard can accompany him." In that moment, I was forced to make a choice: Do I piss off Sir Paul McCartney or the Secret Service by pushing back on their respective stances?

I chose to piss off the less powerful party: the Secret Service. I called the White House social secretary (and an old friend of mine), Julianna Smoot, and she got the director of the Secret Service, Joe Clancy, in the East Room of the White House with Barrie and me, and I begged them to let Paul's bodyguard come to the show, not in the role of a bodyguard, with no weapon, as an audience member.

Director Clancy wasn't budging—he accused us of trying to trick the Secret Service by sneaking the bodyguard on the guest list. I made the only honorable choice: I threw the other executive producer under the bus and said I had no idea he did that (which was true!). And I reassured the director that the bodyguard was not going to be operating as a bodyguard.

Finally, Director Clancy relented; he agreed to let the bodyguard into the show, on the condition that if he acted like a bodyguard, even for a second, he would be kicked out of the White House, banned from all federal buildings, and forced to go through extra layers of airport security for the rest of his life. And I'll tell you what: that was a sacrifice I was willing to make. The bodyguard would be admitted, and the show was back on.

Just before the show, we had all the performers together in the State Dining Room to take pictures with the president. I was in charge of corralling everyone into an organized line so we could get it done as quickly as possible. But of course, everyone was excited and chatting and having fun—exactly the opposite of what you want when you're trying to make something happen in an orderly fashion. Julianna came up to me and said, "If you don't bring order to this, we're going to have to cancel photographs with the president. He's fixing to come down."

That led to one of the most surreal moments of my life. I grabbed a glass, clinked a spoon, and shouted as loud as I could, "Listen up! Stevie Wonder, you're behind Elvis Costello. Elvis, get behind Herbie Hancock. Jonas Brothers, you're first in line because you're first up on the stage." I couldn't believe I was barking orders at a room full of celebrities, but people, like animals, follow the alpha male—or the loud male. Thank God, everyone got pictures with the president.

After the audience arrived for the show, I got the chance to give some remarks welcoming everyone to the East Room of the White House. "I have always dreamt of being Paul McCartney's opening act," I said, "[though] I suspect that this is the smallest venue that Sir Paul has played since The Cavern, back in his early Liverpool days."

I had to acknowledge the historic significance of honoring a Brit at the White House: "We had our first British invasion in 1812 and they burned this house down...and we got over that. We had our second British invasion in 1964 and Sir Paul was one of the ringleaders.... Forty-six years later, tonight's results will be far more entertaining to the residents of this home."

What followed was an absolute onslaught of star power. Jerry Seinfeld performed a hilarious tribute to Sir Paul, which crushed from the opening line: "Mister President, First Lady, Sir Paul McCartney... other people."

Then we got to witness some fantastic performances from an eclectic group of musicians: Jack White, Elvis Costello, the Jonas Brothers, Faith Hill, Emmylou Harris, and Dave Grohl all played renditions of classic Paul McCartney songs.

In an especially touching act, Herbie Hancock accompanied Corinne Bailey Rae in a performance of "Blackbird." It was a song

Paul McCartney and previous Gershwin Prize recipient Stevie Wonder
embrace at dinner at the Library of Congress. They would go on to sing
"Ebony and Ivory" together the next evening at the White House.

Paul McCartney wrote in tribute to the civil rights movement, performed by two Black artists, with the first Black president in the
front row. Another amazing moment came before President Obama's
remarks, when Sir Paul McCartney and Stevie Wonder played their
song "Ebony and Ivory" together. Stevie shared a slightly embellished

version of how they recorded it in the early 1980s: "It was such a joy, Paul, doing that song with you at Montserrat. It was so much fun there…driving cars and flying planes."

In his speech paying tribute to the man of the evening, President Obama spoke about the parallels between Paul and the namesake of the prize: "It's fitting that the Library has chosen to present this year's Gershwin Prize for Popular Song to a man whose father played Gershwin compositions for him on the piano; a man who grew up to become the most successful songwriter in history."

And then Paul proved it by closing out the night with a revue of some of his most famous songs. The first was "Michelle," a song he said he'd "been itching to do at the White House, and I hope the president will forgive me," followed by "Eleanor Rigby," "Let It Be," and, of course, "Hey Jude," which ended with every performer from the night, the first family, and the president coming onstage and singing together. Talk about taking a sad song and making it better.

✦ ✦ ✦

We hosted the Gershwin Prize at the White House two more times: for the songwriters Burt Bacharach and Hal David in 2012 and for Carole King in 2013. Both years made for fantastic shows, with more spectacular performances from Sheryl Crow, Gloria Estefan, and Billy Joel, along with repeat outings from Lyle Lovett, James Taylor, and Stevie Wonder. The president continued to attend, giving the evening an air of significance every year.

But after the 2013 Gershwin Prize, things took a turn. Jim Billington wanted the Library of Congress—and really, himself—to have a bigger role in the prize. So, at his direction, the Library of Congress decided to take on the duties of executive-producing and moved the show out of the White House. At that point, we, the original founders of the prize, decided we didn't want to have anything to do with the new version of the show, and we resigned from our positions as executive producers.

Our names are and always will be on the show as creators, but since 2014, control over the show has belonged to the Library of Congress, and they've since moved the show to the Daughters of the American Revolution Constitution Hall. To me, that's a shame—when you've got a slot at the White House, you should never give it up. The way I see it, Jim Billington let his ego get in the way of what was best for the show, and that meant taking attention away from the president and the White House. In the end, I think it was to the detriment of the quality of the ceremonies and the prestige of the award. At least until 2017. Then the White House spent four years being about as prestigious as the Chuckle Hut in Marble Falls, Texas.

Jim Billington retired from the Library of Congress in 2015 and passed away at the end of 2018. I'm not sure what the future of the Gershwin Prize will be now that its creators are no longer involved. Nevertheless, I am proud of the shows we put together and that we got to create the Gershwin Prize in the first place. Ultimately, the most important outcome of the Gershwin Prize is not where the ceremony takes place, or whose names are in the credits, but that every year, someone who has brought joy to millions of people through their music gets an evening to be honored for the masterful works they've composed.

CHAPTER TWENTY-EIGHT

In Performance at the White House

Since 1978, Washington, DC's premier public broadcasting station, WETA, has produced a recurring program called *In Performance at the White House*. Each event is an opportunity to celebrate a different aspect of American culture—right at the epicenter of American government.

Starting with the Carter administration and continuing on through the Obama administration, WETA would periodically produce these shows, often with the first family in attendance. The first few years of the Gershwin Prize were under the *In Performance at the White House* umbrella, and I first became involved with the series when I produced those shows.

Later, in the waning years of the Obama administration, I also got to be an executive producer for three one-off shows for this series with the help of Dalton Delan at WETA, all of which shined a light on outstanding achievements in American arts.

They were "The Gospel Tradition," celebrating the incredible history of gospel music in the United States; "A Celebration of American Creativity," commemorating the fiftieth anniversary of the National Endowment for the Arts and the National Endowment for the Humanities; and "The Smithsonian Salutes Ray Charles," where, well, the Smithsonian saluted Ray Charles.

As part of my work as executive producer, I delivered welcome remarks for each event in the East Room of the White House. Here are some highlights from my experiences on each show.

✦ ✦ ✦

On April 14, 2015, we gathered in the East Room of the White House to pay tribute to gospel, a foundational American genre. It felt fortuitous, considering the enormous role of Black artists in the genre, that the first Black president of the United States would preside over this retrospective.

But first came my welcome remarks. Also fortuitous, considering I *love* gospel music. "Music is for the ear, but gospel is for the soul," I observed. "But of course, I'm preaching to the choir."[12]

The show had a rock star lineup—or a sacred lineup. We had people of God in Bishop Rance Allen and Pastor Shirley Caesar. We were treated to the gorgeous vocals of Michelle Williams, Tamela Mann, and Darlene Love. We had country singers too—Rhiannon Giddens, Rodney Crowell, Emmylou Harris, Lyle Lovett—representing a genre owing much of its roots to gospel.

Of course, we had President Obama and First Lady Michelle Obama in the front row. I'd call them guests of honor, but technically, we were *their* guests. We *did* have American royalty on the lineup, which I pointed out: "We'll also hear from the legend herself: Aretha Franklin. Think about it! In one room we've got the president of the United States, and the Queen of Soul. Honestly, it took the entire protocol office to figure out who to list first on the invitation."

I kid, but we did do everything in our power to accommodate the needs of Her Souliness, with the help of the great White House Social Secretary Jeremy Bernard. Aretha specifically requested that her surroundings be as warm as possible to create the best environment for

---

12 Forgive me, Father, for I have punned.

her vocal cords. We obliged, and Jeremy turned the air conditioning off before her big entrance. Now, we're talking about a crowded, raucous East Room in Washington, DC, in April. It got hot, and it got hot *fast,* and it stayed that way even as Jeremy turned the AC back on when she took the stage. For a gospel show, it began to feel like an inferno (albeit a fun, happy inferno).

After the space was sufficiently preheated, the voice of God introduced Aretha Franklin, and boy, was that moniker appropriate for this performance. Right off the bat, before uttering a single syllable, Aretha got a standing ovation. Then in an incredible display of show-woman-ship, she stayed in the wings, held her microphone to her face, and started slowly singing, "I Love the Lord, He Heard My Cry," a riveting hymn that instantly consumed the room with joy. My goosebumps had goosebumps. And this was all before Aretha even got up to the stage.

She continued for a full minute before the music kicked in. Then, in she came—weaving through the crowd with a dazzling silver dress and mink coat—to join the Morgan State University choir in a rendition of "Plant My Feet on Higher Ground." She thanked the first family, brought up the Williams Brothers (Doug and Melvin), and they sang a take on "Precious Memories."

As that song came to a tremendous crescendo, Aretha kept belting glorious riffs as she walked toward the piano. She fell to her knees in prayer…and stayed there for a while…until eventually it became clear she wasn't gonna be able to get back up off her knees without a little help.

It was a chaotic moment as we tried to figure out who would help. The White House doctor approached, I stood up, and even the president stood up, but Aretha kept singing as the Williams Brothers and a stagehand came to her aid and "lifted her up." As the song ended, she saved face and got a huge laugh: "Lord lift me…and help me not to get back down on my knees again!"

Incredible: the Queen of Soul was also hilarious. She kept half-singing, "Lord help me up! Y'know, I was sixteen when I was doin' that. I'm not sixteen anymore!"

Soon enough, Aretha acknowledged her fellow performers, then slowly ceded some space on the stage while making direct eye contact with the president, as if to say, "It's all you now, Barack."

President Obama stood up from the front row, ascended to the stage, gave Aretha a kiss on the cheek, took a good look around, and simply observed: "We been to church tonight."

"It feels like old-time religion here," he continued. "Air conditioner broke...women all fannin' themselves...." This got a laugh that can only be described as rapturous. A laugh that transitioned seamlessly into euphoric cheers. A laugh for the ages. A laugh that could heal civilizations.

Then Aretha quipped, "Where are the fans?"

And the president clarified: "That's what the programs are for!"

In the end, Aretha only performed roughly three songs. But in gospel, that's enough for a thirty-minute set. And I say "roughly three songs" because technically the keyboard players never stopped vamping, so who knows when one song ended and another began? Let's retroactively call it a medley. Whatever it was, it was one of the most spiritual experiences I've ever enjoyed.

✦ ✦ ✦

On October 14, 2015, the White House hosted "A Celebration of American Creativity," coinciding with the fifty-year anniversary of the founding of the National Endowment for the Arts and the National Endowment of the Humanities. With no particular genre being honored, we were celebrating American art and literature in general, and there were no holds barred.

As a result, we welcomed a diverse lineup in the East Room of the White House: from blues artists like Buddy Guy and Keb' Mo', to Broadway stars like Audra McDonald and Brian Stokes Mitchell. From jazz musicians like Trombone Shorty and Esperanza Spalding, to singer-songwriters ranging from James Taylor to Usher. From rappers like MC Lyte and Queen Latifah, to actresses like Queen Latifah, to producers like Queen Latifah, to royalty…like Queen Latifah.

Before any of that, there was one diva's performance we had to get out of the way: my opening remarks. I acknowledged the event's distinguished hosts: "Tonight, we celebrate the fiftieth anniversary of the National Endowment for the Arts and the National Endowment for the Humanities. Let's thank the first family for hosting what promises to be another unforgettable performance here at the White House. This is actually a secret part of the first lady's 'Let's Move' initiative. She knows once we hear Usher, none of us will be able to stay in our seats."

In celebrating these agencies, we also acknowledged the president who made them possible: Lyndon B. Johnson. His daughters, Lynda Robb and Luci Johnson, were in attendance.

I expressed the country's gratitude for their father's contributions to America's cultural landscape, while pointing out an apparent contradiction: "Now, Lyndon Johnson was an…*earthy* fellow. He once commented that he'd rather sit down on an old log with a farmer and talk than take in an opera. But he also loved people, and he knew that art, and music, and literature not only brought people together; they were also the purest expression of our humanity."

And I emphasized the variety of works the agencies made possible: "The agencies we celebrate today—the NEA and the NEH—are unique in Washington. As one author put it, they were 'not intended to solve a problem, but rather to embody a hope.' Turning little-known talents like Ken Burns into household names. Giving us Grammy winners, and Pulitzer Prize winners, and those big volumes of history that you keep on your shelf so your friends know how smart you are."

With that, I made everyone turn their phones off ("Neither the NEA nor the NEH has given a grant to create a ringtone—so *we don't want to hear yours*"), and kicked off the show.

Even with so many world-renowned performers on the lineup, President Obama's remarks were a major highlight. He quoted one of that night's acts: "'Listen to the lyrics,' Buddy Guy once said. 'We're singing about everyday life. Rich people trying to keep money, poor people trying to get it, and everyone having trouble with their husband or wife.'"

The president caught himself. "Except me!" he added, to a big laugh. And then he summed up why we were all in that room: "We've got to support our artists, and celebrate their work, and do our part to ensure that the American creative spirit that has defined us from the very beginning will thrive for generations to come."

✦ ✦ ✦

On February 24, 2016, the White House hosted the final *In Performance at the White House* show of the Obama administration: "The Smithsonian Salutes Ray Charles." I had gotten to know the head of the Smithsonian, Dr. David Skorton—and we also met with Richard Kurin, the Smithsonian's acting provost. We knew we wanted to partner together on a music show, and Ray Charles was a natural choice because of the sheer breadth of his impact on American music.

Plus, it was an appropriate bookend: the first White House show of the Obama administration celebrated the music of Stevie Wonder, and now Stevie's "Uncle Ray" was getting his due. Though it'd been over a decade since Ray's passing, his influence on soul, R&B, gospel, jazz, country, and rock & roll remained immutable.

The show featured some of the most prominent singers in gospel, R&B, soul, and blues to be inspired by Ray Charles, including Yolanda Adams, Leon Bridges, Andra Day, Anthony Hamilton, and Jussie Smollett.[13] The Band Perry represented the influence Ray Charles had on country music, while Usher and Demi Lovato reflected Ray's influence on pop. Not to mention one of Ray Charles's contemporaries: Sam Moore of the duo Sam and Dave.

In my welcoming remarks, I mentioned Ray Charles's first visit to the White House: "He met with President Nixon in the Oval Office. In retrospect, that was probably the first time he was recorded here. Of course, that was supposed to be a secret."

I compared this show with our first Obama White House show, getting a laugh and big smile from the president: "We've had Wonder and *Genius*...and everything in between."

I noted the universal praise for Ray Charles. "[He's] been called many things: 'One of the top ten artists of all time.' *Rolling Stone* said that. 'A giant of an artist.' Aretha Franklin said that. 'One of the first great truly American singers.' A saxophonist by the name of Bill Clinton said that. Meanwhile, I'm only being called one thing: the guy keeping us from getting this show started."

And I couldn't help but incorporate a *few* references to Ray's body of work, including but not limited to:

"I'd like to thank the first family for graciously, as Ray would say, 'Bringing Love Around Again' and hosting us this evening."

"Turn off your phones and electronic devices, even if your ringtone is 'What'd I Say.'"

"The incredible performances will no doubt make you want to 'Shake a Tail Feather,' so feel free to move if the mood hits you."

"Finally, it's time for me to 'Hit the road, Cap.'"

After I "Busted" off the stage, the show kicked off with the president delivering some brief remarks. I know. "Here We Go Again." He began: "Tonight's a little bittersweet because this marks our final *In Performance at the White House*."

---

13 Jussie claims he wasn't there, but the overwhelming evidence suggests otherwise.

The crowd sighed in disappointment. Then, more bad news: "I will not be singing."

Then President Obama defined the anatomy of soul by citing our honoree. "Ray fused jazz, gospel, and blues into a new soul sound. As he put it, 'Gospel and the blues are almost the same thing. It's just a question of whether you're talkin' about a woman, or God.'"

I make sure to pray to both, just in case.

Toward the end of the night, Usher educated the crowd about Ray's time at Shiloh Baptist Church, where the preacher would sing, and the congregation would sing right back. He gave fair warning that as he sang "What'd I Say" that he'd be doing the same thing—a call-and-response. Soon enough, everybody was up on their feet with "heys" and "hos" goin' back and forth.

When the song ended, the president got up to thank everybody. And then, a special moment. President Obama closed the night by leading the call-and-response[14] leading into a last reprise, and everybody went wild—or at least, "wild" within standard White House decorum.

However cynical I get about American politics, moments like these give me hope. When you can have the leader of the free world standing side by side with legends of a uniquely American genre, having a blast like it's the only thing that matters...that's *America the Beautiful.*

---

14 An approximate transcript: "Heyyyyyy!" "Heyyyyyy!" "Hoooooo!" "Hoooooo!" "Heyyy!" "Heyyy!" "Hooo!" "Hooo!" "Heyy!" "Heyy!" "Hoo!" "Hoo!" "Hey!" "Hey!" "Ho!" "Ho!" (and so on).

Dueling teleprompters display the remarks of President Barack Obama and Cappy McGarr.

CHAPTER TWENTY-NINE

Navy Seal of Approval

For a few years during the Obama administration, I had the honor of organizing a regional panel to interview prospective candidates for the White House Fellows program. I was asked to do this by the head of the program, Cindy Moelis, at Julianna Smoot's recommendation. Since President Johnson founded the program in 1964, it has let outstanding young people serve as aides to cabinet secretaries and senior staff in the executive branch of the US government.

One year, Janie and I hosted a dinner and invited fourteen candidates from all over the country. One in particular caught my attention. Chris Domencic was a Navy SEAL who served his country for over a dozen years. He was deployed to Iraq twice and Afghanistan four times, and graduated at the top of his class at the US Naval Academy before getting a master's in public policy from Princeton. The kid had chops.

But when we asked the candidates to introduce themselves, Chris surprised me. Everyone played up their accomplishments (with an air of humblebrag), but when Chris stood up, he simply said: "My name is Chris Domencic. I'm in the United States Navy." No brags, humble or otherwise.

I admired his humility. But how the hell was this guy supposed to get hired if he wasn't willing to talk about his incredible life story?

The next morning, Chris was the first to be interviewed by our panel, of which I was the chair. Every question we asked got one of the following two-word responses: "yes sir," "yes ma'am," "no sir," and when he was feeling really wild, "no ma'am."

As I walked Chris out of the interview, the last thing I wanted to tell him was that he was going to lose. But I told him, "Chris, you're going to lose."

"I think your story is incredible," I said. "But you need to *tell* it. Tell them about when you became a SEAL. Tell them about when you got married. I mean, you can tell them about the first time you had sex for all I care. But you've gotta be passionate and show some emotion."

That's when he opened up. "Actually, General So-and-So told me the same thing." (I'm leaving out the general's name so I don't end up on some kind of watchlist.)

"Look at me," I said. He did. "You're a f**king namedropper."

Chris burst out laughing. His shoulders finally dropped, and he thanked me for the advice.

We sent only Chris to final interviews with the President's Commission. One of the commission members was a soft-spoken public servant himself: Senator Tom Daschle. He called me and said, "I think you'll like our pick. Your guy from the Dallas panel is going to be a Fellow."

I was ecstatic. But it became a little bit more complicated. Chris became an aide to the secretary of commerce, John Bryson. But shortly thereafter, Bryson took a leave of absence after suffering a seizure. For the time being, the department would be run by an interim secretary.

Around that time, I invited Chris and his wife, Rachel, to be my guests at that year's Mark Twain Prize honoring Ellen DeGeneres. There, I asked Chris how he was doing.

He confessed: "I'm stuck in a cubicle with no windows, and it feels like my job doesn't matter. I clock in at 7:00 a.m. I clock out at 7:00 p.m. The interim secretary hasn't asked me to do one thing."

I was upset to hear the program wasn't serving his needs. So I sprang into action. I called Senator Daschle and asked if I could call some folks at the West Wing to get Chris transferred there.

Ever honest, Tom responded, "Absolutely not. You'll hurt your reputation. Every White House Fellow wants to be in the White House. You'll hurt his chances of promotion. Don't do it."

I took Tom's advice and kept my mouth shut. But I wasn't happy about it. A couple weeks later, Cindy Moelis called to ask if I would put the panel together again for the following year. I was "noncommittal," or at least, "sure as hell not going to do it without venting to Cindy first."

I told her about Chris's situation. I eventually agreed to put together another panel. But what would be the point if the folks we fought for weren't getting to do real work?

Another few weeks passed, and I received a phone call from Chris. He was effusive: "I just wanted to thank you. I'm in the West Wing of the White House, and I'm reporting to Gene Sperling, director of the National Economic Council."

He explained that Senator Daschle and Cindy Moelis told him I had something to do with his reassignment and let me know it was a much better fit. I was so glad to hear it. I was also glad I had somehow gotten credit for it, when I really just dumped my emotions on Senator Daschle and Cindy Moelis—something I'll do anytime.

Later on, Chris became the aide to General Martin Dempsey, who was Obama's chairman of the Joint Chiefs of Staff. Chris called me and said, "You need to come to my change of command."

I took his orders. I went to the Little Creek Navy base in Virginia Beach for Chris's change of command to take over the Naval Special Warfare Development Group (or as it's known to you and me, SEAL Team Six.) It was one of the most heartwarming moments I've ever witnessed…until the ceremony when he left that post a couple years later.

I got former Navy Secretary John Dalton to give the keynote, and Chris shared farewell remarks. He thanked his team, Secretary Dalton, his family, and finally, "my mentor, Cappy McGarr."

I have to admit, I teared up pretty good that day. But when I greeted Chris after the ceremony, I told him: "Nope, I can't call myself your mentor. But consider me your campaign manager."

I've never met anyone with Chris's integrity, humility, heart, discipline, and dedication to his country. Getting to be in his corner was a privilege in itself. And yes, that is a humblebrag.

Cappy McGarr and Navy SEAL Commander Chris Domencic.

CHAPTER THIRTY

Afterthoughts

Photos by up-and-coming photographer/author Cappy McGarr.

"Mark Twain is perhaps the most erroneously
quoted figure in human history."
—OSCAR WILDE

I live a funny life. It's funny because it's unbelievable. I've met nine US presidents, and what's more, I managed not to make an ass of myself in front of any of them.[15] I grew up seeing Hollywood stars on TV and in movies, only to find myself face-to-face with them, decades later, in the halls of the Kennedy Center. I was born the son of a roughneck, but I've never worked an oil rig, and my neck couldn't be smoother.

It's funny because it's ironic. When I was young, dumb, and full of, uh, chewing gum, I seriously thought about moving to Los Angeles to pursue standup comedy. If Councilman Lebermann hadn't knocked some sense into me, I may never have had a career in finance, and ultimately, I never would have had the chance to co-create the Mark Twain Prize. Giving up comedy ended up being the best decision I ever could have made for my comedy career.

It's funny because it's true. I'm constantly interrupting myself with the refrain, "I'm not makin' this up!" "Cappy" isn't a nickname; it's really on my birth certificate. I really yodeled with Carol Burnett at the Folger Shakespeare Library. I really putted on the Eisenhower Green at the White House with Bill Murray.

It's funny because, frankly, it's jam-packed with funny people. Of course, there are the comedians I've had the privilege of meeting. Richard Pryor, Whoopi Goldberg, Steve Martin, Tina Fey, Ellen DeGeneres, Carol Burnett, Bill Murray, David Letterman, Julia Louis-Dreyfus, Dave Chappelle—the list goes on and on and on.

And by far, I've shared the most laughs with family. My mother-in-law, Annette Strauss, was as funny as she was charming as she was brilliant. Janie and the kids crack me up every time we're together. Kathryn, in particular, is both funnier than I am *and* published a book before I could. Hell, my grandson Hud has been around for just a couple years, and he's already a laugh riot.

---

15 For those of you keeping score: that's Johnson, Nixon, Carter, Reagan, Bush 41, Clinton, Bush 43, Obama, and Biden. Nixon was the only one I didn't get a picture with. Just another off-the-record meeting, I guess.

Then, against all odds, the politicians I've met have been some of the funniest people of all. Ann Richards came up with the most quotable one-liners I ever heard. Lloyd Bentsen had a devastatingly dry deadpan. President Obama was quick on his feet and had an arsenal of dad jokes at his disposal. Lowell Lebermann was qualified to advise me against standup comedy because he had a heightened sense of humor himself.

Those folks were particularly inspiring to me because they employed humor in the pursuit of public service—to persuade people to do the right thing or to come around to an idea. The best comedy leaves you thinking after you're done laughing.

✦ ✦ ✦

We're coming up on a quarter-century of the Kennedy Center Mark Twain Prize, spanning four presidents, three decades, two TV networks, and one mission: to honor the greatest contributors to American comedy of our time.

And just as important as the honoree or the esteemed guests is the venue. Unlike the president, the Kennedy Center is unimpeachable. As the foremost cultural institution in the United States, when we give comedians the respect they deserve as artists and thinkers, it sends a message. Comedy isn't just a distraction or folly; it's a fundamental through line of American culture. It's what gets you through your day during the bleakest moments. It's a pointed form of free speech that can reveal the truth and expose hypocrisy.

Sometimes, it can feel like there's not much to laugh about. Late night talk shows can become more cathartic than comical. At one point, the president stopped showing up to the White House Correspondents' Dinner, and then they stopped inviting comedians. Even the Oscars can't always find a host who won't make everybody upset.

With all of these institutions fraying at the edges, the Mark Twain Prize has never been more important. We need to know it's okay to laugh, and we need the people who make us laugh to be recognized. As long as the Mark Twain Prize is around, we'll get that yearly reminder and tribute from the nation's capital.

And I know the Mark Twain Prize will persevere, because it has endured dire times before. The initial idea was brought to the Kennedy Center because the Clinton White House was too enveloped in scandal to host a comedy show. We honored Whoopi Goldberg just weeks after the September 11 attacks, when nothing made sense, and no one felt funny. We survived both 2016 *and* 2020, for God's sake.

All of this isn't to say that the Mark Twain Prize will always look exactly the way it does now. We'll keep reformatting it and tinkering with it as time goes on. Just as the comedians we honored twenty years ago may be considered controversial today, we could find that twenty years from now, our sensibilities have changed again. That's okay: comedy changes.

But while comedy might change, being funny has always stayed the same. You have to read the room. You have to surprise people. You have to speak truth to power. The room changes; the people change; even the truth changes. But from the dawn of humanity to our bitter end—2050ish?—laughter has been and always will be one of the greatest joys we can experience. A joy that brings us together.

If I've done nothing else—and the jury's still out—let it be known that I spent the better part of my life making an effort to share that joy with the world.

Whether I'm chatting some guy up at a fundraiser or producing a show celebrating a legendary comedian for millions to see, I'm always looking to get the next big laugh. Sometimes I get it; sometimes I don't. But I'd like to think that in some small way, with every joke, I've made the world a better, happier, funnier place.

That said, I don't want to overstate it. After all, you've gotta stay humble when you're the man who made Mark Twain famous.

APPENDIX A

Why Washington Needs a Laugh

In the years since we started the Mark Twain Prize, its necessity has become clearer and clearer. With every election cycle, the country gets more divided, the political discourse gets nastier, and faith in our political institutions fades a little bit more.

I believe that humor is a key tool in our fight against these disturbing trends. If you can get people to laugh with each other and at themselves, they'll see each other as human and be that much closer to common ground.

In 2011, I got together with my friend Jeff Nussbaum, now a speechwriter for President Biden, and a longtime funny guy who has been a creative consultant for the Mark Twain Prize, and we wrote an op-ed about the crucial role that humor can and should play in politics.

It's still relevant today. If anything, I think it resonates more given what's transpired in American politics in the years since.

✦ ✦ ✦

The Kennedy Center on Sunday hosts the 14th Annual Mark Twain Prize for American Humor—our national award for humor. It honors people who have had an impact on American society in ways similar to Mark Twain, the perceptive social commentator and satirist who helped America laugh at its leaders and itself. This year's honoree will be Will Ferrell.

At last year's event, for Tina Fey, Steve Martin said this was a night when Washington becomes a comedy Mecca. He paused a beat. "And," Martin continued, "we all know how funny Mecca is."

Like all great humor, his joke stemmed from truth.

Why is it that Washington evokes all sorts of laughter, but does so little laughing itself?

In part, it's because troubling times usually cause someone to claim that mirth is passé, or inappropriate, or just over.

But Jon Stewart was closer to the mark when he said, after Sept. 11, "A country that allows for open satire [demonstrates] the difference between closed and open. The difference between free and…burdened."

And Washington could use some unburdening.

Humor in Washington has always been fraught—usually regulated to a very limited time and place.

That time? In the first three minutes of a speech.

And the place? A select group of dinners, like the Gridiron Club, and a cluster of correspondents banquets, where politicians are expected to poke fun at themselves and others.

There is a reason that members of Congress—of both parties—are held in lower public esteem than ever before. The political discourse is so rancid, and the players seem so unlikable. Humor could help alleviate both.

But humor, a social lubricant and general elixir of likability in so many other facets of life, seems to make few appearances in the life of Washington.

This is in part why Mo Udall called his autobiography *Too Funny to be President*. (We'll leave it to political scientists to tell us whether this was his only electoral stumbling block.)

It's in part why Bob Dole, famously funny behind closed doors, seemed dour in public. He published his book *Great Political Wit* only after he left office.

The best humor does two things: First, it says with a smile things hard to say with a scowl. Second, it walks right up to the line of propriety.

The challenge—and the risk—is that sometimes you only see the line once you've crossed it.

Witness President George W. Bush, in 2004, at a radio and television correspondents' dinner, narrating a slideshow in which the running gag was his inability to find weapons of mass destruction. Senator John Kerry (D-Mass) called it a "stunningly cavalier" attitude toward a war that was costing U.S. lives—and he was right.

But you know who else was not funny? Kerry. In 2006, when he was considering seeking the presidency again, he flubbed a joke so badly it virtually ended his candidacy. Speaking to college students in California, Kerry said, "You know, education—if you make the most of it—you study hard, you do your homework and you make an effort to be smart, you can do well. If you don't, you get stuck in Iraq."

A few words, but a far cry from his intended—and still not funny—punchline: "You end up getting us stuck in a war in Iraq. Just ask President Bush."

A group of soldiers delivered the coup de grace, posing with a banner: "Halp us Jon Carry. We R stuck hear n Irak."

Ironically, while Bush and Kerry showed the risks of comedy, it was the soldiers who got it right. Humor is a powerful weapon. But to turn it on others, you need to demonstrate the ability to turn it on yourself. If you can laugh at yourself, you've earned the right to laugh at others.

And even as you take aim at others, take heed of the Gridiron Club mantra: Humor should singe but not burn.

The rewards can be great. Witness Bill Clinton expertly lampooning (and so overcoming) his end-of-term doldrums with a fantastic "last days" video. Or how the humor in Alaska Governor Sarah Palin's 2008 convention speech ("The difference between a hockey Mom and a pit bull? Lipstick!") made her, momentarily, likable and relatable.

Still, with the chilling effect of flubbed jokes on serious topics, official Washington has fled from an attempt at laughter—and that's a problem.

Abraham Lincoln at the height of the Civil War, asked his cabinet, "Gentlemen, why don't you laugh? With the fearful strain that is on me night and day, if I did not laugh I should die, and you need this medicine as much as I do."

Lincoln was ahead of his time. A recent report, in the Proceedings of the Royal Society B: Biological Sciences, has now established a causal sequence between laughter and endorphin activation. In other words, they've established why laughing until it hurts…doesn't hurt.

Last year, at a Friar's Club Roast of Quentin Tarantino, which supports the Wounded Warriors Gift of Laughter Program, Cappy, who chaired the luncheon, approached a soldier who was in a wheelchair, and had also lost an arm, to thank him for his service, and for attending the event.

The soldier looked up at him. "When I laugh," he said, "I don't hurt."

There is so much hurting in our nation right now, and so much standing in the way of progress. We need to laugh more. We need to heed Twain's timeless adage: "Against the assault of laughter, nothing can stand."

APPENDIX B

A Brief History of American Comedy

I fell in love with comedy at a young age, and I haven't stopped since. But I first grew to truly appreciate the work that comedians do in college, when I wreaked havoc on the radio waves of KNOW as Goober Hoedecker, the confrontational country bumpkin who harassed the likes of Austin's city council members and even the mayor.

I've come to realize that in our small way, our show was building off of the long history of comedians pushing boundaries and mocking people in power—sometimes, directly to their face.

I want to talk about how comedy originated as an underappreciated genre of performance—and eventually became mainstream enough for the people in power to acknowledge it, and even participate in it.

When I was in college, *Saturday Night Live*'s debut was still a couple of years away—just a twinkle in Lorne Michaels's eye. Johnny Carson was the undisputed king of late night. Richard Pryor had just put out his first couple of albums, and he was co-writing *Blazing Saddles* with Mel Brooks.

Today, we rightly list names like these as cultural icons. But comedy hasn't always held a venerated role in American society; it certainly wasn't the type of "art" that would be celebrated by our nation's leaders at places like the White House or institutions like the Kennedy

Center. That's because comedy has much more of an underground origin story.

At its best, comedy is the language of underdogs, who slowly work their way up from seedy venues to the national stage. In America, comedy itself has followed a winding path to the mainstream, beginning with the slapdash days of vaudeville.

Across the country at the turn of the twentieth century, thousands of performers in hundreds of venues performed countless wildly theatrical acts—singing and dancing and magic and, yes, comedy. Acts like Charlie Chaplin, the Marx Brothers, Buster Keaton, Bob Hope, and Burns and Allen got their start traveling around the country to perform as part of variety shows in theaters of varying prestige to audiences of varying backgrounds.

Most comedy routines in vaudeville shows looked like what we now call sketch comedy: multiple performers playing big characters with quippy wordplay and slapstick punchlines.

Often, the lines blurred between comedians and musical acts. The Marx Brothers, for example, began as a musical group called the Nightingales. According to Stefan Kanfer's biography of Groucho Marx, pursuing comedy was an afterthought when the brothers realized that riffing as the act went wrong got a better reaction from the audience than the act itself.

And before Jack Benny became one of the country's biggest radio and TV stars, he started as a violinist. Like the Marx Brothers, he stumbled upon humor as a performance asset when a throwaway joke between songs elicited big laughs from the crowd. He described that moment as a turning point: "The sound intoxicated me. That laughter ended my days as a musician, for I never again put the violin back where it belonged except as a gag."

Soon enough, some acts broke the mold by doing something revolutionary: walking on stage with nothing more than a suit and a microphone, and telling jokes straight to the audience. On purpose! Often rehearsed beforehand!

At some point during this period, the first stand-up comedian emerged. Some comedy historians credit Frank Fay with "pioneering the emcee." As one of the first vaudeville hosts at the Palace in New York City, he set an example for how a performer could demonstrate value simply by directly addressing the audience.

In the book *The Comedians: Drunks, Thieves, Scoundrels, and the History of American Comedy*, Kliph Nesteroff reveals how even basic rules of hosting a comedy show were breakthroughs on Fay's part: "His role as an introducer and extroducer was another revolutionary shift in stand-up. He wasn't just introducing, but entertaining as he did so. If the previous act bombed, he warmed the crowd back up, and if the momentum was good, he just kept the show going."

While some early stand-ups broke the mold of vaudeville, others embraced its style. Take Henny Youngman (please). After years of watching broad, high-octane acts in vaudeville houses, he developed an electrifying act with nothing more than his words: Youngman became known as the King of the One-Liners, telling as many jokes as he could in as little time as possible.

Beyond their escapist roles, stand-up and vaudeville could also be platforms for underrepresented people to express themselves. In particular, two historically marginalized groups carved out a niche in the early days of stand-up: Black and Jewish Americans.

Jewish performers thrived in the Borscht Belt—a constellation of summer resorts in the Catskill Mountains of upstate New York. (It was coined the Borscht Belt by Abel Green of *Variety*, after the soup that the hotels often served at lunch.) This circuit ended up being a haven for comedians like Milton Berle, Mel Brooks, Lenny Bruce, Sid Caesar, Rodney Dangerfield, Estelle Getty, Jerry Lewis, Jackie Mason, Carl Reiner, Don Rickles—and this list is heavily abridged.

In an interview with *Time* magazine, Yiddish language professor Jeremy Dauber explained that the Borscht Belt's heavily Jewish audience allowed Jewish comedians to put on acts that were, well, more Jewish—using Yiddish language, incorporating personal stories, commenting on Jewish culture—telling jokes that might not have played as well in front of a gentile-heavy nightclub crowd. Then, when those same comedians hit it big with national television appearances, the influence of the Borscht Belt spread to the mainstream of American comedy.

Meanwhile, Black performers toured the Chitlin' Circuit. These were performance venues around the country (especially in the South) where it was considered safe for Black musicians and comedians to perform at the height of the Jim Crow era. (In a play on the Borscht Belt, the Chitlin' Circuit was named for the soul food that venue kitchens would serve.)

After traveling city to city developing their acts in front of local Black audiences, many of the performers went on to achieve national success. In particular, Jackie "Moms" Mabley broke new ground over and over again, becoming the first woman comedian to perform at the Apollo Theater in Harlem, having her debut album *The Funniest Woman in the World* become gold-certified, and eventually performing on *The Ed Sullivan Show* and the Carnegie Hall stage.

Lots of other pioneering Black comedians stopped by the Chitlin' Circuit, including Redd Foxx, Dick Gregory, Dewey "Pigmeat" Markham, Richard Pryor, Nipsey Russell, Jimmie Walker, Slappy White, and Flip Wilson.

Through vaudeville and stand-up, both Black and Jewish performers got to perform in front of sympathetic crowds, subverting and embracing stereotypes on their own terms.

Around the same time that stand-up comedy spun off into its own genre, the troupes of vaudeville made their way to radio, and millions of listeners who may have never seen a live show became familiar with its performers and those they influenced.

Of course, vaudeville stars couldn't just throw their acts on the air and call it a day. These performers were used to repackaging the same material over and over for different live audiences around the country. So, comedians had to learn how to use the medium to their advantage as they were tasked to constantly fill new hours, week after week.

Eddie Cantor was among the vaudeville stars who learned to adapt to radio's format. Having proved himself with long runs at variety houses across the country and starring in several of Broadway's famous Ziegfeld Follies (one of the most iconic theatrical revues of the period), Cantor gradually navigated his way toward success in broadcasting.

It took time and experimentation for him to decide whether to perform broadcasts in front of a live audience (he eventually did), whether to bring on other comics and stars (yes), and whether to air segments making fun of the show's sponsor (absolutely). These innovations led Cantor's jokes and songs to reach a wider audience than he could have dreamed of as a live performer, as he hosted various radio shows from the 1930s through the 1950s: *The Chase and Sanborn Hour*, *Time to Smile*, *The Pabst Blue Ribbon Show*, and *The $64 Question*, to name a few.

Radio also allowed vaudeville performers to set an evocative scene with minimal production value. A duo like Abbott and Costello could blow listeners away with a routine like "Who's on First?" as they used the tools of broadcasting to parody sports commentary.

Of course, in adapting traditions from vaudeville, some performers also brought along racist stereotypes that pervaded early performances. Such stereotypes would be the bedrock of one of the all-time most popular and long-running radio programs: *Amos 'n' Andy*. Broadcast for the first time in 1928, white performers Freeman Gosden and Charles Correll played a pair of Black caricatures in one of the earliest comedic serials. The radio program ran for over thirty years, beginning on local Chicago station WMAQ and eventually being broadcast by NBC and CBS to a nationwide audience. For all of its outmoded tropes, *Amos 'n' Andy* was one of the earliest examples of a comedy series with continuously new (if not fresh) material.

By the mid-1930s, the vast majority of American households had a radio, and it became the anchor of home entertainment. Performers like Jack Benny, Bob Hope, and Fred Allen became household names as they hired staffs of writers to churn out material for their variety shows. Because of the immediacy of the medium, comedians could fill their shows with topical humor without worrying about its expiration date. And while *Amos 'n' Andy* was at the peak of its popularity, *The Jack Benny Program* became the first nationwide radio broadcast to feature an African American in a regular role, with Eddie Anderson playing Benny's valet, Rochester.

Going into the 1940s and 1950s, as Americans brought home their first televisions, many popular comedy shows came straight from radio. Some hosts adapted programs that had already achieved widespread success; others fled to TV as safe harbor after failed experimentation with radio.

Another former vaudevillian, Milton Berle, spent about a dozen years—from 1936 to 1949—hopping from one radio program to the next. In his *Encyclopedia of Old-Time Radio*, author John Dunning calls him "radio's best-known failure: never able to mount a decent rating despite numerous attempts in many formats." But the final radio program he hosted, *Texaco Star Theater*, made the leap to television in the fall of 1948 as one of the first comedy-variety shows on the air—and it was a near-instant hit. His show was credited by the *New York Times* for the rapid expansion of television stations and sets in the late 1940s, and soon "Uncle Miltie" became "Mr. Television"— practically synonymous with the medium.

Meanwhile, after thriving on radio for more than two decades, *The Jack Benny Program* made its network debut on CBS in 1950 and aired hundreds of episodes over the next fifteen years. Around the same time, George Burns and Gracie Allen brought their show to CBS too, racking up a dozen Emmy nominations over the next decade. And Steve Allen, who hosted a nightly radio program called *Smile Time,* went on to host several TV shows over the years, including a new NBC late-night venture called *Tonight.*

Variety shows like *The Tonight Show* would become a destination for club comics to make their television debut and reach a national audience, especially after Johnny Carson took the reins from Jack Paar in 1962. Future legends like Joan Rivers, George Carlin, Bill Cosby, and Steve Martin built their audiences through frequent appearances (and guest hosting stints) that would lead to many opportunities to headline their own projects down the road.

Johnny Carson himself became the gold standard for the late-night comedy host, tucking Americans into bed with topical monologues, ridiculous sketches, celebrity interviews, stand-up sets, and musical performances—and becoming a key influence for multiple generations of young comedians who have become the titans of American comedy today.

And, although nobody has yet called me a titan of American comedy, I was watching too. Growing up, I was influenced by the comedians I saw on TV and listened to on the radio. I collected albums from Shelley Berman, Bob Newhart, and Vaughn Meader. I watched every Marx Brothers and Mel Brooks movie religiously. I adored duos like Burns and Allen, Abbott and Costello, and even—wait for it—Rocky and Bullwinkle.

These comedians (and anthropomorphic animals) shared one trait I love: they pushed the envelope. I was always most excited by the mischievous pranksters who would run right up to the line (and occasionally cross it). *Especially* the ones who did this directly to powerful people, like the comedic impressionists who used radio and TV to impersonate and satirize politicians.

In the early years of radio, when humorist Will Rogers experimented briefly with impersonating then-Presidents Calvin Coolidge and Franklin D. Roosevelt, he had to issue apologies because some of his listeners couldn't tell the difference between his impression and the real thing. According to historian Peter Robinson, it was difficult for many Americans to imagine someone ridiculing the office on the airwaves like Rogers did.

It got easier to imagine. Vaughn Meader came a couple of decades later. A stand-up comedian who grew up in New England, Meader developed a nightclub act in the early 1960s impersonating President John F. Kennedy. That led to *The First Family*, a sketch comedy album featuring seventeen tracks centered around his impression (and Naomi Brossart's Jackie Kennedy.)

The album was a phenomenon. It sold more copies more quickly than any other album in history at the time—not just comedy albums, but albums, period—1.2 million in the first two weeks of release. It won Album of the Year at the 1963 Grammys—another major achievement, joining *The Button-Down Mind of Bob Newhart* as one of the only comedy albums to get that honor. Maybe the most important recognition came from President Kennedy himself, who responded: "I enjoyed Mister Meader's album very much. But I really think he sounds more like Teddy."

After Kennedy was assassinated, Meader's career crashed faster than it skyrocketed. Still, he made his impact, getting millions of Americans to adore the idea of the political impressionist.

Political impressions would become a calling card of *Saturday Night Live*. Originally known as *NBC's Saturday Night*—because ABC already had a show called *Saturday Night Live* hosted by sports journalist Howard Cosell—Lorne Michaels pitched the show as one of the network's first live outings since the 1950s. (About two decades had passed since Sid Caesar's *Your Show of Shows* went off the air, which would have been the closest comparison.)

As Lorne reflected later, an experimental sketch show was seen by executives as risky. With every idea he pitched, he was told "it'll never work in prime time." Instead, they made it work at 11:30 p.m. on Saturday, with the original cast aptly called the Not Ready for Prime Time Players.

One of *SNL*'s most famous traditions is the presidential impressionist. With every new administration comes an iconic new mimic: think Chevy Chase as Gerald Ford, Dan Aykroyd as Jimmy Carter, Phil Hartman as Ronald Reagan, Dana Carvey as George H. W. Bush, Darrell Hammond as Bill Clinton, Will Ferrell as George W. Bush, Fred Armisen and Jay Pharoah as Barack Obama, and Alec Baldwin as that guy that came after Obama.

These impressions have shaped Americans' perceptions of the presidents, for better or for worse (let's face it, usually worse). But they also give their targets the opportunity to humanize themselves by being a good sport about it.

Just as Kennedy issued a good-natured response to Vaughn Meader, Ford took Chevy Chase's pratfalls in stride, even making an appearance on the show from the Oval Office. Dana Carvey had a close friendship with Bush 41. And President Trump…well, he regularly watched the show. Not everyone avails themselves of the good publicity that comes from standing side by side with your satirist, but, amazingly, that has become an American tradition in itself, echoed by the White House Correspondents Dinner (when everyone shows up) and the countless late night talk shows that welcome politicians as guests.

The Mark Twain Prize was created in that same spirit. Every year, a comedy legend comes to Washington, is invited to meet the president, and is recognized by the Kennedy Center—our National Cultural Center. It shows that as a nation, America has a sense of humor. We don't silence people who mock our institutions; we celebrate them. At least, that's how it should be.

APPENDIX C

Pure Vanity

If you're reading the appendix, you probably know: I've got more stories than I could fit into one book. Some were pivotal moments with major implications in the history of comedy and politics. And some…are just fun. My foray into country music falls squarely into the latter category.

Around my fiftieth birthday, I grabbed dinner at Bob's Steak & Chop House with my old college roommate and lifelong buddy Bob Kaminski.[16] There, Bob asked me a question any fifty-year-old just *loves* to hear: "Do you have any regrets?"

To his surprise, I responded instantly: "Yes—I haven't recorded my country album."

Bob balked. I couldn't tell if he was surprised that I *wanted* to record a country album or that I *hadn't already*. Sure, I wasn't technically a country singer, so I had no business recording a country album. But how do you become a country singer? By recording a country album![17]

I told Bob that I even had a title in mind that reflected the seriousness of the project: *Pure Vanity*. And shockingly, he seemed interested in helping make it happen. "Listen, if you give me the songs you want to sing, maybe that'll be your birthday present."

---

16 Just to keep things as confusing as possible, Bob Kaminski has no relation to Bob Kaminsky or Bob's Steak & Chop House.

17 *Ipso facto, country singo, stroké ego.*

It was a nice gesture, but we moved on and I didn't really think much of it. The next day around two in the afternoon, Bob called me up and asked for my playlist. And in fact, Bob had called nine of my friends to contribute to the cause and help produce the CD.[18]

I chose eight songs that, in my mind, represent an abridged history of country music:

1. "High Time (You Quit Your Low Down Ways)"
— Waylon Jennings & Billy Ray Reynolds

2. "Half as Much" — Hank Williams Sr. & Curley Williams

3. "Waiting for a Train" — Jimmie Rodgers

4. "Hobo's Meditation" — Jimmie Rodgers

5. "Honky Tonkin'" — Hank Williams Sr.

6. "Heaven and Hell" — Willie Nelson

7. "Why Don't You Love Me" — Hank Williams Sr.

8. "Mule Skinner Blues" — Jimmie Rodgers & George Vaughn

For four weekends, I went into a recording studio and busted out renditions of all these tunes. I was accompanied by some legitimate country artists—sorry, some *fellow* legitimate country artists. We had Mike Gage on drums, bass, and backup vocals; Mark Robinson on lead guitar; Jeff Williams on keys and fiddle; and Junior Knight on steel guitar. (And Cappy on pipes.) All of these guys were total professionals who had played with music legends, like Ray Wylie Hubbard, Ray Price, LeAnn Rimes, and many others.

---

18 Here's the full list of *Pure Vanity's* executive producers: Bob Dedman, Jeff Doumany, Tom Erickson, Jack Furst, Bob Kaminski, Bob Lutz, Mark Langdale, Don McNamara, Bill Miller, and Bill Noelke. For those of you keeping score, that's 30 percent "Bobs," 20 percent "Bills," and 50 percent "other."

Once we printed the album art, I had to include a warning label beneath the track listing:

WARNING: Please do not attempt to listen to this CD unless you have had at least one pack of beer or one bottle of 1959 Chateau Latour. If you find yourself breaking into random fits of yodeling and are not able to stop, call Yodelers Anonymous at 1-800-555-YODEL.[19] *Do not attempt to operate heavy machinery while listening to this CD.*

Pure Vanity became an instant hit among megalomaniacs named Cappy McGarr. I got piles of copies to give out as party favors at my fiftieth birthday party for anyone who would take them. (Guests were required to take them.)

A few weeks later, Mark Pryor came to Dallas for a lunch I was hosting during his first campaign for US Senate. He saw the stacks of *Pure Vanity* on my desk, insisted he had to hear it, and took a copy. He was in my target demo: country enthusiasts who know me personally.

I like to think that even now, all these years later, former Senator Mark Pryor still has *Pure Vanity* cued up in his pickup truck. Precisely where it belongs.

The cover and liner notes for underappreciated country
album Pure Vanity by Cappy McGarr.

---

19 I've been trying to make that my personal number for *years*.

Believe it or not, *Pure Vanity* is not my greatest contribution to the world of country music.

After my first term at the Kennedy Center was finished, I joined the National Archives Foundation Board, and one of their distinguished historians was Ken Burns.

You know Ken Burns. He's the documentarian behind amazing retrospectives like *The Civil War*, *Baseball*, and *Jazz*. After I met him, I learned that he was also an upstanding guy who would laugh at my jokes. We've been inseparable ever since.

After the 2008 recession, a lot of Ken's sponsors backed out of supporting his work, so I helped him start The Better Angels Society, a nonprofit that raises funds for his documentaries.

Soon thereafter, Ken was staying with Janie and me in Dallas, and we took him out to dinner. He doesn't drink; that's why I think he's so brilliant. I drank wine; that's when I think I'm brilliant. As such, I started to pitch my brilliant creative friend one of my brilliant unsolicited ideas.

I told him: "Ken, you oughta do the history of American music."

And he replied: "I've already done that with *Jazz*."

I pushed back: "Okay, but Ken, you know most people don't like jazz." Now, I like jazz myself, but I just wanted to mess with him and see how he would respond.

Here's how: "You have no idea what you're talking about, do you?"

"Probably not," I conceded, "but you haven't done the history of country music."

I outlined all the key figures that would need to be in the series. Ken listened politely. After I laid out the pitch, he said, "Well, that's interesting," which usually means "Let's move on, Cappy."

The next day, while I was cooking breakfast, Ken came down to the kitchen, and told me: "Hey, I called Dayton Duncan," one of Ken's most frequent collaborators, "and we're doing country."

At dinner, it was a crazy idea; by breakfast, it was greenlit. It took Ken another decade to get it made. But it happened: *Country Music* debuted on September 15, 2019, on PBS. It got a nice write-up in *Rolling Stone*, where Ken shared the idea's genesis. You know where this is going.

Here's the quote from *Rolling Stone*: "Ken Burns was in Dallas some years ago visiting a good friend, philanthropist Cappy McGarr. The filmmaker was working on his 2012 Depression-era miniseries, *The Dust Bowl*, and as usual for a workaholic who often has six or seven films brewing, Burns was turning over ideas for his next project. When McGarr suggested tackling country music, 'It just *exploded* in my brain—like, *of course*,' Burns says. 'And as we got into it, we saw that it was as real, important, and emotionally compelling as any film we've made.'"

It was very thoughtful of Ken to give me credit for that conversation, especially since he knows as well as anyone that I was going to share that *Rolling Stone* clip with everyone on my contact list. In fact, our mutual friend and AOL co-creator Steve Case emailed the both of us to warn about what Ken had done: "If you keep giving Cappy credit, he will be insufferable."

Joke's on him. I was planning on being insufferable whether I got credit or not.

ACKNOWLEDGMENTS

*F*irst, to my fellow Texan, Chandler Dean: it has been a true pleasure working with you. Laughs, laughs, and more laughs. This writing project—or egomaniacal scrawl, whatever you want to call it—would not have been possible without your skill, patience, and humor. It has taken over two years to assemble my thoughts and writing into a(n) (in)coherent narrative, but it has been a pleasant journey. I do hope that the readers of this book (all seven of you!) get as much pleasure reading or listening to it as I have recounting some of these great adventures.

Second in paragraph order, but tied for first in my heart, I would also like to thank Jeff Nussbaum for helping me put my thoughts and musings down on paper for years now. I have known Jeff since he was in his twenties, and he has been a close friend ever since. When I am at a loss for words, he seems to always come up with the right ones.

I want to thank my friend Ken Burns, both for writing the wonderful foreword for this book about humor, and for humoring me, in general, in every one of our delightful conversations over the years.

Thanks to Mark Ulriksen for his spectacular illustration of Twain's caricature (and mine!) on the book's cover. I'm so happy that after illustrating over fifty *New Yorker* magazine covers, he has finally upped his game with this project.

I also want to thank my literary agent Jan Miller and her colleague Austin Miller for taking on the little book that could, and guiding me to Post Hill Press. Of course, thanks to Heather King, Debra

Englander, and the team at Post Hill Press for helping me navigate the whole publishing process.

And thanks to Luke Dempsey and Jay Hodges for providing edits with candor and helping get this book into great shape.

To Drew Patrick, my astute and brilliant confidant and lawyer: thank you for (patiently) guiding me through all contracts. You always give excellent, thoughtful advice. William Shakespeare once said "kill all the lawyers"—to which I say: Okay, but please, let's save Drew!

A special shout-out to my late mother-in-law, Annette Strauss. She was the first woman ever elected as mayor of Dallas, as well as the first Jewish person elected mayor. And when she wasn't smashing glass ceilings, she was opening doors for me at the Kennedy Center and the University of Texas. In fact, she was the type to open doors literally and figuratively—she was both polite *and* well-connected.

I would never have pursued a presidential appointment to the Kennedy Center if Annette hadn't exposed me to the institution in the first place. Bob Strauss (her brother-in-law, and one of my mentors) got President Carter to appoint Annette to the Kennedy Center, and she took Janie and me to their events many times, including a number of Kennedy Center Honors. She also lobbied for me to serve on the University of Texas Development Board, where I later served as chair of the board.

She left us over twenty years ago, but in her memory, my granddaughter is aptly named Annette. (And her middle name is "Cap," which I'll graciously accept as an honorable mention.)

Next, a huge thank you to Larry Wilker, Ann Stock, John Schreiber, Mark Krantz, and Murray Horwitz. I spoke to them often about how the Mark Twain Prize began, from its initial conception as a White House show, to the fateful meeting in Larry Wilker's office that started it all. I joined the team at that meeting, as did Peter Kaminsky, and he was soon followed by his brother, Bob, who brought his extensive experience in TV production to the table.

John Schreiber and Murray Horwitz knew Dalton Delan at WETA, who came on as an executive producer when the show moved from Comedy Central to PBS. He has been a champion for the Mark Twain Prize ever since.

After my Clinton-appointed term at the Kennedy Center ended in 2002, it was Mark Krantz who suggested that I continue to work on the Mark Twain Prize as an executive producer along with the Kaminsky brothers. Years later, the four of us received our Emmy nomination for the show honoring George Carlin. Mark is a kind and thoughtful man.

Michael Matuza has assisted in booking the talent for most of the shows in the later years of the Mark Twain Prize and the *In Performance at the White House* series. Michael and I also worked with the Friars Foundation to produce a show at the Kennedy Center dedicated to military veterans called The Lincoln Award, recognizing organizations and individuals who have supported veterans. Michael is a delight to work with and, for what it's worth, he has exceptional contacts in the entertainment industry.

After twenty-two great years (and counting), thanks to the hard work of all of these people and many others, the Mark Twain Prize has become firmly established as an institution for the Kennedy Center.

The Mark Twain Prize would never have happened without Will Ris, the former senior vice president of government affairs for American Airlines. In the early days of the Twain, I called Linda Daschle, who, I should mention, is a former FAA acting administrator and recipient of the Glen A. Gilbert Memorial Award for outstanding achievement in aviation, which is on display at the Smithsonian's National Air and Space Museum. (Translation: she just plane knows her stuff.) I asked her if she knew of an airline that could fly in talent for the Mark Twain Prize ceremony. She introduced me to Will, and because of his efforts, American Airlines has generously supported every Mark Twain Prize and every White House show I produced. They still sponsor the Twain to this day.

Also, it would be remiss of me if I didn't mention that Linda Daschle is as pretty on the inside as she is on the outside. If you don't believe me, she's got the credentials to back it up. I swear this is true: she represented Kansas in the Miss America pageant and won Miss Congeniality! She's not just beautiful and kind…she is *certifiably* beautiful and kind.

Additionally, I want to make sure to mention some other stalwart supporters of the Mark Twain Prize from the Kennedy Center family who were there at the beginning: Jim Johnson, Marie Mattson, Ambassador Jean Kennedy Smith, Buffy Cafritz, and Alma Powell. Though they might have been somewhat skeptical about the idea at first, they came around and have become some of the Twain's most dedicated advocates. Shout-out as well to Leslie Miller and Matthew Winer who have been incredibly helpful to the Mark Twain Prize throughout the years.

The chairman of the Kennedy Center, David Rubenstein, is probably the most outstanding philanthropist I have ever met. He is brilliant, kind, and a generous leader. His vision has not only improved the Kennedy Center, but also almost every institution in Washington you could think of. The United States is lucky to have a committed citizen like David who believes in his country, and who is at the forefront of "patriotic philanthropy," a term he coined. Unlike "compassionate conservatism," it's actually a real thing.

Over the years, the president of the Kennedy Center has played a key role in the Mark Twain Prize, though some have been more aggressively supportive than others. Larry Wilker was the one who greenlit the show in the first place, and there's simply no way it would have gotten off the ground without him. Larry was followed by Michael Kaiser, who oversaw the Twain for over a decade.

I have long been a strong proponent of the principle that the Kennedy Center should own the Mark Twain Prize. After all, it's called the *Kennedy Center* Mark Twain Prize. But for years, the Kennedy Center only owned one-third of the show, with the other two-thirds split between the Kaminsky brothers and Mark Krantz. After Deborah Rutter became the president of the Kennedy Center in 2014, she finally started negotiating the buyout of Krantz and the Kaminskys. ("Krantz and the Kaminskys" is my favorite Lenny Kravitz cover band, incidentally.) Bob was negotiating on their behalf, and Deborah couldn't quite get a yes out of them, so I assisted in the process and helped close the deal.

Now, the Kennedy Center owns 100 percent of the Mark Twain Prize, as it should be. You wouldn't want to abbreviate the Krantz Kaminsky Kennedy Center Mark Twain Prize.

From the world of politics: the late Lloyd Bentsen, the longtime senator from Texas, introduced me to Tom Daschle when Tom was still just a candidate for Senate in South Dakota. Tom and his wife have become two of Janie's and my closest friends.

I have to thank Tom for all the incredible opportunities that he has afforded me, including but not limited to: assisting my presidential appointments to the Kennedy Center, taking me to eleven State of the Union addresses, and getting me a ticket to watch the impeachment trial of President Clinton and to hear the president's 1999 State of the Union address *that same day.* As I have said over and over again, throughout this book and to whoever will listen in-person, Tom Daschle is one of the most outstanding public servants I know—if not *the* most.

In my life, I've been lucky to make a number of very close friends. One of my closest friends is David Perry, whom I talk to and laugh with every day. If you only end up with one friend like David, that is a life well lived. I'm also close with David's brother Richard, and

Richard's wife, Lisa. In fact, Richard is my daughter Elizabeth's godfather. The Perrys are kind and generous friends all around.

In my book, humor is the mark of any great friendship, and that's certainly the case with my friends Jeff Doumany, Berry Cox, Ryan Bell, David Jaderlund, and Bob Kaminski. I always look forward to getting together with them—and there is always laughter involved.

Most importantly, I would like to thank my wife, Janie, and my daughters, Elizabeth and Kathryn. Humor has always been an essential part of our lives. From those precious nights sitting around the dinner table as the kids grew up to the unforgettable family trips where we did our best to keep each other entertained, and every moment in between—it's been one long, ongoing contest to determine who's the funniest.

(And by the way, the results are in: it's Kathryn.)

Speaking of family, I have to mention my mother, Carolyn, my biggest fan, who did me one of the greatest favors of my life by insisting I get a great education at St. Mark's and the University of Texas.

Finally, I'd like to close these acknowledgments with one last reason I wrote this book. I have two grandchildren as of this writing, Annette Cap and Hudson Michael McCue. I wanted to make sure they knew about some of the unbelievable people I've met and institutions I have been involved with. I've been fortunate enough to be a founder of the Kennedy Center Mark Twain Prize for American Humor, and a creator of the Library of Congress Gershwin Prize for Popular Song; I've also had the privilege of presiding over years of Mark Twain Prize rehearsal dinners—in the National Statuary Hall at the Capitol, in the Benjamin Franklin Room at the State Department, at the Smithsonian, twice in the Supreme Court, and several times in the Renwick Gallery. Not to mention welcoming guests to the East Room of the White House for music shows featuring Paul McCartney, Stevie Wonder, Carole King, and Aretha Franklin, among so many others!

It has been quite the ride. And it's still going. But if you want to find out what wild experiences life is going to throw at me next… you'll have to buy the next book. Tentatively titled: *The Man Who Made* The Man Who Made Mark Twain Famous *Famous*.

Cappy McGarr, Steven Wright, and Jerry Seinfeld.

Cappy McGarr and Lily Tomlin.

Dick Gregory, Trevor Noah, Cappy McGarr, and Janie McGarr.

Carol Burnett, Cappy McGarr, and Julie Andrews.

NAME DROP DIRECTORY

FOREWORD

Huckleberry Finn

Ulysses S. Grant

Lyndon B. Johnson

Cappy McGarr

Janie McGarr

Theodore Roosevelt

George Bernard Shaw

Mark Twain

PREAMBLE

Lloyd Bentsen

Joe Biden

Mel Brooks

Bill Clinton

Tom Daschle

Tina Fey

Aretha Franklin

Al Gore

Jimmy Kimmel

Steve Martin

Paul McCartney

Eddie Murphy

Bill Murray

Barack Obama

Martin Short

INTRODUCTION: DELIRIOUS IN THE OVAL OFFICE

CHAPTER ONE: EVERYBODY READY, EXCEPT CAPPY

CHAPTER TWO: APPARENTLY FAIRLY BRIGHT

CHAPTER THREE: AS GOOBER GOES, SO GOES THE STATION

CHAPTER FOUR: BLIND LEADING THE BLIND

CHAPTER FIVE: AN UNIDENTIFIED AIDE

Pete Geren
Yo-Yo Ma
Jack Martin
Janie McGarr
Barack Obama
Dan Quayle
Ann Richards
Bob Strauss

CHAPTER NINE: LANDSLIDE DASCHLE

Lloyd Bentsen
George H.W. Bush
Bill Clinton
Tom Daschle
Nancy Erikson
Rita Lewis
Jack Martin
Ross Perot
Ross Perot, Jr.
Elizabeth McGarr McCue
Kathryn McGarr

CHAPTER TEN: FOLLIES, LEGISLATIVE AND RABBINICAL

Larry Amoros
Dolph Briscoe
Janey Briscoe
Tom Daschle
Sue Fischlowitz
Steve Gutow
Arsenio Hall
Ann Richards

Joe Lieberman
Graham Nash
Stephen Stills

CHAPTER FOURTEEN: THE MARK TWAIN PRIZE

Lenny Bruce
Buffy Cafritz
William Cafritz
Jimmy Carter
Dave Chappelle
Bill Clinton
Hillary Clinton
Katherine Dunham
Morgan Freeman
Whoopi Goldberg
Murray Horwitz
Jim Johnson
Bob Kaminsky
Peter Kaminsky
Elia Kazan
Jim Kimsey
Mark Krantz
Monica Lewinsky
Marie Mattson
Janie McGarr
Alma Powell
Colin Powell
Leontyne Price
Richard Pryor
Ronald Reagan
Carl Reiner

Chris Rock
John Schreiber
Jerry Seinfeld
George Shultz
Frank Sinatra
Jean Kennedy Smith
Jimmy Stewart
Ann Stock
Annette Strauss
Virgil Thomson
Dick Van Dyke
Paul Warfield
Damon Wayans
Larry Wilker
Robin Williams
Jonathan Winters
Stevie Wonder

CHAPTER FIFTEEN: WINTERS IS COMING / CARL'S HOUR

Sid Caesar
Bill Clinton
Tina Fey
Karl Gerhardt
Steve Martin
Mary Tyler Moore
Richard Pryor
Carl Reiner
Charlie Reiner
Rob Reiner
Jerry Seinfeld
Jean Kennedy Smith

Donald Trump
Robin Williams
Jonathan Winters

CHAPTER SIXTEEN: WE CAN STILL BE FUNNY

Harry Belafonte
George W. Bush
Cedric the Entertainer
Billy Crystal
Linda Daschle
Tom Daschle
Tommy Davidson
Whoopi Goldberg
Alan King
David Letterman
Janie McGarr
Lorne Michaels
Conan O'Brien
Caroline Rhea
Paul Simon
Wanda Sykes
Jon Stewart
Chris Tucker
Bruce Vilanch
Robin Williams

CHAPTER SEVENTEEN: BROADCASTING LEGENDS OF BROADCASTING

Dan Aykroyd
John Belushi
Richard Belzer

George W. Bush
Earl Campbell
Dave Chappelle
Tim Conway
Jack Crosby
Joanne Crosby
Jane Curtin
Ellen DeGeneres
Chris Dodd
Jacob Epstein
Tina Fey
Kelsey Grammer
Darrell Hammond
George Lopez
Bernie Mac
Steve Martin
John McCain
Lorne Michaels
Willie Nelson
Bob Newhart
Dolly Parton
Miss Piggy
Mary Kay Place
Don Rickles
Darrell Royal
Edith Royal
Paul Simon
Elaine Stritch
Julia Sweeney
Lily Tomlin
Christopher Walken

CHAPTER EIGHTEEN: HOPES DASCHED

George W. Bush
Bill Clinton
Tom Daschle
Tim Johnson
John Kerry
Barack Obama
John Thune

CHAPTER NINETEEN: A TEXAN AND TWO NEW YORKERS

Jason Alexander
Christina Applegate
Lucie Arnaz
Matthew Broderick
Mel Brooks
George W. Bush
Sid Caesar
Samuel Clemens
Bob Costas
Billy Crystal
Larry David
Robert De Niro
Danny DeVito
Richard Dreyfuss
Jimmy Fallon
John Goodman
Tom Hanks
Patricia Heaton
Eric Idle
Diane Keaton
Anthony Kennedy

Nathan Lane
Queen Latifah
Jon Lovitz
Steve Martin
Lorne Michaels
Randy Newman
Robert Redford
Carl Reiner
Rob Reiner
Martin Short
Neil Simon
Paul Simon
Lily Tomlin
Barbara Walters

CHAPTER TWENTY: TRAGEDY AFTER TRAGEDY IN COMEDY

Richard Belzer
Lewis Black
George Carlin
Kelly Carlin
Margaret Cho
Bill Cosby
Jimmy Durante
Peter Kaminsky
Jimmy Kimmel
Ben E. King
Denis Leary
Bill Maher
Richard Pryor
Michel Richard
Joan Rivers

Garry Shandling

Jon Stewart

Lily Tomlin

CHAPTER TWENTY-ONE: TWAIN IN THE TWEENS

Fred Armisen

Ed Asner

Jack Black

Matthew Broderick

Carol Burnett

George W. Bush

Steve Carell

Johnny Carson

Kristin Chenoweth

Tom Daschle

Ellen DeGeneres

Jimmy Fallon

Will Ferrell

Tina Fey

Aretha Franklin

Jon Hamm

Sean Hayes

Jennifer Hudson

Lyndon B. Johnson

Jimmy Kimmel

Jane Krakowski

John Leguizamo

Jane Lynch

Jacqueline Mars

Steve Martin

Janie McGarr

Adam McKay
Seth Meyers
Lorne Michaels
Tracy Morgan
Jason Mraz
Barack Obama
Conan O'Brien
Viveca Paulin
Nancy Pelosi
Amy Poehler
Sam Rayburn
Mitt Romney
Pete Rouse
Paul Rudd
Molly Shannon
Taylor Swift
Lily Tomlin
Vince Vaughn
Betty White
Owen Wilson

CHAPTER TWENTY-TWO: THE ONE THAT GOT AWAY

Mel Brooks
Dave Brubeck
Grace Bumbry
Robert De Niro
Whoopi Goldberg
Carl Reiner
David Rubenstein
Deborah Rutter
Bruce Springsteen
Robin Williams

CHAPTER TWENTY-THREE: CAROL BURNETT AND THE CAR BOY

Julie Andrews
Tony Bennett
Joe Biden
Garth Brooks
Carol Burnett
Johnny Carson
Kristin Chenoweth
Hillary Clinton
Tim Conway
Kevin Eubanks
Jimmy Fallon
Tina Fey
Chelsea Handler
Rashida Jones
Kourtney Kardashian
Robert Klein
Vicki Lawrence
Jay Leno
Al Madrigal
Kate McKinnon
Seth Meyers
Barack Obama
Amy Poehler
Steve Ricchetti
Robert Risko
David Rubenstein
Maya Rudolph
Jerry Seinfeld
Martin Short
J. B. Smoove

Wanda Sykes
Bruce Vilanch
Rosemary Watson

CHAPTER TWENTY-FOUR: THE COUP OF BILL MURRAY

Aziz Ansari
Jay Bernhardt
Roy Blount Jr.
George M. Cohan
Jane Curtin
Miley Cyrus
Brian Doyle-Murray
Merrick Garland
Rhiannon Giddens
Bill Hader
Craig Johnson
Clayton Kershaw
Jimmy Kimmel
David Letterman
Janie McGarr
Lorne Michaels
Bill Murray
Barack Obama
Antonin Scalia
Paul Shaffer
Frank Sinatra
Emma Stone
Sigourney Weaver

CHAPTER TWENTY-FIVE: THE KING OF LATE NIGHT AND THE QUEEN OF SITCOMS

Louisa May Alcott
Stephen Colbert
Bryan Cranston
Larry David
Chris Elliott
Tina Fey
Al Franken
Ilana Glazer
Tony Hale
Biff Henderson
Abbi Jacobson
Alan Kalter
Brett Kavanaugh
Keegan-Michael Key
Jimmy Kimmel
Lisa Kudrow
David Letterman
Mike Lotus
Julia Louis-Dreyfus
Norm MacDonald
Steve Martin
Paul McCartney
John Mulaney
Bill Murray
Kumail Nanjiani
Barack Obama
Amy Schumer
Jerry Seinfeld
Paul Shaffer
Martin Short

Donald Trump
Eddie Vedder
Jill Vedder
Jimmie Walker
Warren Zevon

CHAPTER TWENTY-SIX: CHAPPELLE'S PRIZE

Aziz Ansari
Erykah Badu
Yasiin Bey
Dave Chappelle
Michael Che
Common
Bradley Cooper
Morgan Freeman
Tiffany Haddish
Colin Jost
John Legend
Steve Martin
Lorne Michaels
Trevor Noah
Q-Tip
David Rubenstein
Sarah Silverman
Jon Stewart
Kenan Thompson
Frédéric Yonnet

CHAPTER TWENTY-SEVEN: THE GERSHWIN PRIZE

Yolanda Adams
Marc Anthony

Burt Bacharach
Corinne Bailey Rae
Tony Bennett
James H. Billington
Wayne Brady
Joe Clancy
Shawn Colvin
Elvis Costello
Sheryl Crow
Hal David
Dalton Delan
Jerry Douglas
Gloria Estefan
Stephen Foster
Art Garfunkel
George Gershwin
Ira Gershwin
Philip Glass
Dave Grohl
Herbie Hancock
Emmylou Harris
Faith Hill
Dixie Hummingbirds
India.Arie
Anita Johnson
Jonas Brothers
Bob Kaminsky
Carole King
Diana Krall
Mark Krantz
Alison Krauss
Ladysmith Black Mambazo

John Lennon
Lyle Lovett
Stephen Marley
Barrie Marshall
Martina McBride
Mary Mary
Paul McCartney
Lorne Michaels
Barack Obama
Jerry Seinfeld
Paul Simon
Julianna Smoot
Esperanza Spalding
George Stevens Jr.
James Taylor
Jack White
Will.i.am
Stevie Wonder
Buckwheat Zydeco

CHAPTER TWENTY-EIGHT: IN PERFORMANCE AT THE WHITE HOUSE

Yolanda Adams
Bishop Rance Allen
Jeremy Bernard
Leon Bridges
Ken Burns
Pastor Shirley Caesar
Ray Charles
Bill Clinton
Rodney Crowell
Andra Day

Dalton Delan
Aretha Franklin
Rhiannon Giddens
Buddy Guy
Anthony Hamilton
Emmylou Harris
Luci Johnson
Richard Kurin
Queen Latifah
Demi Lovato
Darlene Love
Lyle Lovett
Tamela Mann
MC Lyte
Audra McDonald
Janie McGarr
Brian Stokes Mitchell
Keb' Mo'
Sam Moore
Barack Obama
Michelle Obama
Lynda Robb
David Skorton
Jussie Smollett
Esperanza Spalding
James Taylor
Trombone Shorty
Usher
Michelle Williams
Stevie Wonder

CHAPTER TWENTY-NINE: NAVY SEAL OF APPROVAL

John Bryson
Tom Daschle
Ellen DeGeneres
John Dalton
General Martin Dempsey
Chris Domencic
Martina McBride
Cindy Moelis
Barack Obama
Julianna Smoot
Gene Sperling

CHAPTER THIRTY: AFTERTHOUGHTS

Lloyd Bentsen
Joe Biden
Carol Burnett
George H.W. Bush
George W. Bush
Jimmy Carter
Dave Chappelle
Bill Clinton
Ellen DeGeneres
Tina Fey
Whoopi Goldberg
Lyndon B. Johnson
Lowell Lebermann
David Letterman
Julia Louis-Dreyfus
Steve Martin
Hudson Michael McCue

Janie McGarr
Kathryn McGarr
Bill Murray
Richard Nixon
Barack Obama
Richard Pryor
Ronald Reagan
Ann Richards
Annette Strauss
Oscar Wilde

APPENDIX A: WHY WASHINGTON NEEDS A LAUGH

George W. Bush
Bill Clinton
Bob Dole
Will Ferrell
Tina Fey
John Kerry
Steve Martin
Jeff Nussbaum
Jon Stewart
Quentin Tarantino
Mo Udall

APPENDIX B: A BRIEF HISTORY OF AMERICAN COMEDY

Fred Armisen
Dan Aykroyd
Alec Baldwin
Jack Benny
Milton Berle
Shelley Berman

Mel Brooks
Naomi Brossart
Lenny Bruce
Burns and Allen
George W. Bush
Sid Caesar
Eddie Cantor
George Carlin
Johnny Carson
Jimmy Carter
Dana Carvey
Charlie Chaplin
Chevy Chase
Bill Clinton
Charles Correll
Howard Cosell
Bill Cosby
Elvis Costello
Jeremy Dauber
John Dunning
Frank Fay
Will Ferrell
Gerald Ford
Redd Foxx
Estelle Getty
Freeman Gosden
Abel Green
Dick Gregory
Darrell Hammond
Goober Hoedecker
Bob Hope
Stefan Kanfer

Buster Keaton
Jerry Lewis
Jackie "Moms" Mabley
Dewey "Pigmeat" Markham
Steve Martin
Marx Brothers
Groucho Marx
Jackie Mason
Vaughn Meader
Lorne Michaels
Kliph Nesteroff
Bob Newhart
Barack Obama
Jack Paar
Jay Pharoah
Richard Pryor
Ronald Reagan
Carl Reiner
Don Rickles
Peter Robinson
Rocky & Bullwinkle
Will Rogers
Franklin D. Roosevelt
Nipsey Russell
Donald Trump
Jimmie Walker
Slappy White
Flip Wilson
Henny Youngman

APPENDIX C: PURE VANITY

Ken Burns
Steve Case
Bob Dedman
Jeff Doumany
Dayton Duncan
Tom Erickson
Jack Furst
Mike Gage
Ray Wylie Hubbard
Bob Kaminski
Bob Kaminsky
Junior Knight
Mark Langdale
Bob Lutz
Janie McGarr
Bill Miller
Don McNamara
Bill Noelke
Ray Price
Mark Pryor
LeAnn Rimes
Mark Robinson
Jeff Williams

ACKNOWLEDGMENTS

Julie Andrews
Ryan Bell
Lloyd Bentsen
Carol Burnett
Ken Burns

Buffy Cafritz
George Carlin
Berry Cox
Linda Daschle
Chandler Dean
Dalton Delan
Luke Dempsey
Jeff Doumany
Debra Englander
Aretha Franklin
Dick Gregory
Jay Hodges
Murray Horwitz
David Jaderlund
Jim Johnson
Michael Kaiser
Bob Kaminski
Bob Kaminsky
Peter Kaminsky
Carole King
Mark Krantz
Lenny Kravitz
Marie Mattson
Michael Matuza
Paul McCartney
Annette Cap McCue
Hudson Michael McCue
Janie McGarr
Carolyn McGarr
Kathryn McGarr
Elizabeth McGarr McCue
Austin Miller

Jan Miller
Leslie Miller
Trevor Noah
Jeff Nussbaum
Drew Patrick
David Perry
Alma Powell
Will Ris
David Rubenstein
Deborah Rutter
John Schreiber
Jerry Seinfeld
Jean Kennedy Smith
Ann Stock
Annette Strauss
Bob Strauss
Lily Tomlin
Mark Ulriksen
Larry Wilker
Matthew Winer
Stevie Wonder
Steven Wright